After Hours
Adventures of an International Businessman

by Gene Myers

Copyright © 2009
All rights reserved – Gene Myers

No part of this book may be reproduced or transmitted in any form or by any means, graphic, electronic, or mechanical, including photocopying, recording, taping, or by any information storage retrieval system, without the permission, in writing, from the publisher.

Strategic Book Publishing
An imprint of AEG Publishing Group
845 Third Avenue, 6th Floor - 6016
New York, NY 10022
www.StrategicBookPublishing.com

ISBN: 978-1-60860-074-8
SKU: 1-60860-074-2

Printed in the United States of America

Book Design: Rolando F. Santos

Contents

Foreword vii

Chapter 1
The Rookie 1

Chapter 2
Guaymas 21

Chapter 3
Around the World in Forty Days 41

Chapter 4
Weekend Excursion 73

Chapter 5
Saddam's Guest 83

Chapter 6
The Operation 93

Chapter 7
Germs, Contamination, and Disease 105

Chapter 8
The Kingdom 117

Chapter 9
After Hours in KSA 125

Chapter 10
The Last Cult 131

Chapter 11
Class of '58 Lounge 145

Afterword 163

*For Kay who made coming
home the best journey of all*

Foreword

THE ESCAPADES that follow are true. Rather than present the usual or conventional oft-told account of a business manager engaging in (and overcoming) typical and atypical problems and challenges, I chose mostly to dwell on events that happened outside of a business context. Plainly speaking, this is not a business book.

To state the obvious, there are numerous business books advising one what to do and what not to do to be successful, and just as many suggesting how to turn dismal failure into life-changing achievement, each highlighting the author's quixotic road to victory. Another of that ilk serves no one, especially me. Although I once authored such a book, I must admit I find most pretentious, repetitious, and boring—except mine, of course.

What I tried to provide herein is what Paul Harvey titles one of his radio segments as *The Rest of the Story*; the sometimes inane, off-the-wall consequential and inconsequential things that just happened. These unplanned experiences are not exclusive to me; they happen to every one of us in one form or another. But we just consider them briefly, perhaps enjoy a you-had-to-be-there chuckle, and return to normalcy.

Foreword

Now, please do not misunderstand. I was very devoted to my profession and focused on success for the enterprise and myself. It wasn't until later that, upon reflection, I discovered the real "gold" in my life came from relationships with people and memorable, serendipitous circumstances, not business.

Several of the incidents border on the good taste/bad taste barrier, whatever that is, and I'll do my best to warn you in advance about such events so you may skip those chapters if you desire. But also understand this was life simply unfolding, and as it did, I developed opinions and/or thoughts about such incidents, and chose not to apply any filters as I recorded them. I mean, c'mon, try as we might, we cannot edit life.

Chapter 1

The Rookie

DID YOU ever have one of those jobs that started with joyful anticipation, but after a year or so ended in disappointment? It's not an uncommon tale what with some poor souls claiming a string of frustration that continued a lifetime. You know the type: always bitching about their situation, that they're smarter than everyone else (including the boss), and under appreciated. I may be more fortunate than most, but I had only one such regret, and this is that story.

My first employment opportunity out of college turned out to be that account, but that's not to say it was a bad experience—just one of life's lessons. It began on a positive note, with an additional halo effect that usually accompanies a new event is one's life; that is, there was the excitement of beginning my career in pleasant surroundings which included my anticipated *a priori* model of how my professional life would be shaped. It was energizing and heady. The job required suit and tie and was located at a downtown skyscraper amid big city bustling energy and classy bistros. Lovely professional ladies scurried about during lunch hour and hung out at nearby lounges af-

Chapter 1: The Rookie

ter work. A company car came with the job, because most of the time I would be visiting clients in their factories and office buildings. A nice beginning, wouldn't you say?

Then there was a lovely young lady working her way through college who lived in the apartment building next door. As I stood out front one sunny Saturday afternoon, she came strolling by eating a small bag of potato chips. I could tell by her glance before she entered the building that she took a fancy to me. More on that later, but for now, let me explain how my journey into the world-of-work began.

Like most final semester college seniors I ventured into the campus placement office and reviewed the roster of visiting prospective employers. Many of my classmates signed up for a dozen or more interviews, but I opted for only three. I preferred to attend graduate school, but my anemic bank account pretty much dictated that I find a job. Anyway, most employers paid for graduate school; it's just that it would take much longer.

Here's another thing: I didn't know what I wanted to be when I grew up. I really didn't. My major was mechanical engineering, which I selected because I thought it would open doors to the most opportunities, especially those in manufacturing companies, which were booming with no end in sight. At least, that's what I told myself. With the benefit of hindsight, I think I was just putting in time waiting for some great "aha" moment. We, including parents, career guidance counselors, and teachers, had a myopic worldview during the 50's and 60's. There was engineering, accounting, teaching, medicine, and law—nothing else! The latter two took forever in the mind of an immature eighteen-year-old, and the others seemed boring. I liked English and history. "Impractical," said the adults in my life. My math and science grades were good enough to pursue engineering. They said, "Do that!" So I did.

I showed up for the interviews immaculately groomed and dressed including highly polished shoes. We were told that nice shoes were the first thing looked for by those who hired.

Years later as a senior executive, I was in Boston assisting my sales director, at his request, as he interviewed candidates for a sales manager position. One bright fellow had a combination of glibness, background, and industry knowledge that, in my mind, made him ideal for the job. I recommended my colleague hire him.

He looked at me aghast. "Are you kidding? Did you see that guy's shoes?"

The first interview was with a foundry division of a major automobile corporation. The interviewer introduced himself and offered me a hand to shake. It was a bit strange. He tucked his right elbow into his waist as he extended his hand, palm up, and sort of hunched over like a vulture. His grip was soft and feminine. He offered me a seat at a small table while he sat and squinted at my meager resume.

"I see you worked for Campbell's," he said.

"Yes sir. Summer job."

"And just what did you do for Campbell's?" He looked up and smiled.

"I made V8."

"Excuse me?"

I launched into the aspects of the job and what I did… a sudden memory filled my mind as I droned on about the aspects of the job and my heroic endeavors.

There were these two hillbillies that would show up at my spice mixing station near the end of my shift—second shift. When I was busy, they liked to grab my knife, which I used to slit open one-hundred pound bags of salt, and throw it at the wooden ceiling about

Chapter 1: The Rookie

thirty feet above. When they succeeded, they laughed uproariously. There were probably a dozen knives stuck above my head. These mental giants worked third shift, with an army of their ilk, cleaning the whole damn place with high powered steam hoses.

One night, they failed to show up—much to my pleasure. I found out two nights later one was dead and the other in jail. The guy in jail thought it would be funny to goose his buddy with a steam hose.

The interviewer listened patiently, but without much interest to my various summer job descriptions then launched into a diatribe about cupolas and pig iron. Like him, I didn't have much interest, and it probably showed. He rose abruptly and offered me his hand in the same strange manner. "Thanks for coming in," he said breezily. "We really prefer industrial engineers."

I wanted to ask why he wasted his time and mine, but just thanked him instead.

The second interview, with a major manufacturer of data processing machines, went about the same way. Like the automotive foundry, the likely career path seemed to offer mostly engineering department drudgery with little opportunity to escape. Later, I had to smile at my naïveté. I mean, what did I expect? I studied engineering and those companies offered engineering jobs.

However, the third meeting hit the spot. The company had three regional offices, one on each coast and the third in Chicago. They sought field engineers to visit with factories and offer help designing, installing, and testing various types of physical plant hydraulic systems—rather a combination consulting and sales engineering occupation. A car and an expense account came with the job. Now that was more like it. Upon graduation I was hired and assigned to Chicago.

I took the train from my hometown to Chicago dressed in suit and tie. People dressed to impress when they traveled then. I remember it was a warm, sunny Sunday, and I left about noon. The trip was lonely, but I still fantasized about what was on the other end. The first thing I did after leaving my hotel to find a restaurant was buy a pack of cigarettes, Lucky Strikes. Professional people lit up, right? State Street was only a few blocks away and there I found a lounge called The Rialto Crossroads. Professional people had cocktails before dinner, right? The place was crowded, surprising to me because it was Sunday, but I found an empty stool and ordered a gin and tonic.

I became aware of someone on my right slightly leaning on me. I stole a furtive glance in the mirror behind the bar, wanting to be cool, but ruined the effect by an immediate chin-dropping, open-mouthed, bugged-eyed double take. She was a knockout, dressed provocatively, and smelled of a delightful scent.

"Hi, my name's Betty," she said, touching my arm. It almost seemed like an electric shock.

I gulped. Why would someone like that talk to me? "H-hello," I choked.

She smiled. "I'm a dancer," she added. I imagine she was thinking, "What a rube," but I didn't know about that type of lady then. "You're cute," she said, fingering my hair.

I was scared shitless. "S-so are you," I said haltingly and immediately felt like an idiot. Why not just say uh-hyulk, I castigated myself.

"Buy me a drink?"

"Um, okay."

She flagged down a knowing bartender. "Champagne cocktail." It arrived in warp speed.

Chapter 1: The Rookie

Champagne cocktail? My radar was immediately engaged. I smelled a rat. In fact, I looked around and spied six or so other attractive girls at the bar, each with a champagne cocktail leaning on a chump like me. I'd been had. She picked up on it, and rearranged my hormones by suddenly kissing me. Uh-oh, an instant chubby tried to shut down my alarm system.

She picked up the cocktail and said, "Let's go back to a booth."

"Duh, okay." I knew better, but followed anyway.

She laid a couple more kisses on me, slurped down her drink in two chugs, and made eye contact with someone behind me. Immediately, a matronly waitress arrived with a full bottle of champagne.

Chubby disappeared. I rose and said, "Good-bye, Betty," and walked out the door, bracing for an imagined assault by a bouncer. I was relieved to be outside, but felt like… well, remember those old cartoons where this dumb ass turns into a lollipop labeled "sucker" with a trombone wah-wah-wah in the background? Like that!

I thought my assignment was Chicago, but I was only there for a week of orientation, then sent off to Detroit. Detroit was alive and vibrant, bursting with success and promise for the future.

I had occasion to return to Detroit several years ago and was shocked by what I saw. I stayed at the ultra-modern Renaissance Center on the Detroit River, and traveled by People Mover to Greek Town for dinner. The route took me through the heart of downtown Detroit; through Grand Circus Park, Cadillac Square, and right past Cadillac Tower, where I worked on the thirty-eighth floor. The place was a literal ghost town, the buildings, cafes, department stores, and hotels deserted. Trash blew through the streets, windows were bro-

ken, and the gray pallor of death hung over the immense area that was the Detroit I once knew.

The first day in the office I was assigned to a 37-year-old veteran, Dick, who showed me the ropes. We spent most of the first month at various GM, Ford, Chrysler, and Wyandot Chemical factories. We reviewed piping diagrams for underground water systems, conducted acceptance tests for fixed-pipe carbon dioxide fire retarding systems, and helped design and test fire pump applications. I liked the work. We went to someplace new almost everyday. Although most of our work was in metropolitan Detroit, we also covered the eastern half of Michigan. We worked almost exclusively with plant engineering departments, but always had access to the plant manager as well.

Once a week, usually Friday, Dick and I went to the Cadillac Tower office to be vetted, with the other field engineers, about the week's activity, and turn in our expense accounts. Those were "free days" in that we didn't do much work. The whole office partook in long lunches at the Checker Bar & Grill, featuring great hamburgers and cold beer. After hours, we prowled the nearby lounges en masse looking for whatever it is guys look for in those places. Sometimes one of us succeeded, but usually not me. I managed to collect a lot of phone numbers for the weather, stock quotes, the time, and other places interesting. The ladies were a lot smarter than us—one of us anyway.

Enter Sylvia, my potato chip chomping neighbor. I returned to my apartment early one warm August day, and parked at a rare open spot in front of the building. Usually, I parked in the rear in an assigned slot. I emerged from the car necktie loosened, carrying my suit coat over my shoulder a la Frank Sinatra, a large roll of engineering drawings carried casually in the other hand, and wearing my hardhat. I thought I looked pretty cool. I guess Sylvia did too. She walked up to

Chapter 1: The Rookie

me with a forlorn young man in tow, looked me in the eye, and stuck out her hand.

"Hi, I'm Sylvia, and this is my friend Richard." He was a short chap, poorly dressed, with unkempt hair and beard, doing his best to look bohemian. She, on the other hand, was quite attractive—willowy body, long, straight blond hair, and pouty mouth.

I rearranged my burden, and shook their hands. "Gene," I said. Richard averted my eyes, and looked like he wanted to disappear. "What's the problem, Rich?" I asked.

"Oh, he's an artist," said Sylvia. "And having a bad time."

Rich said, "I gotta go," and walked away, giving a half-hearted wave. I think he had designs on Sylvia, but didn't want to compete with me; me being so cool.

"What do you do?" Sylvia asked—actually more of a demand.

"I'm an engineer."

She rolled her eyes and kind of smirked like I was some kind of low life.

"Something wrong with being an engineer?" I said with an amused twinkle. Man, I was Cary Grant cool.

"Engineers have little class; have no understanding or appreciation of life. Most can't even spell their own name," she stated like she really believed it.

"I got straight As in English," I smiled, enjoying the moment. "And just what do you do?"

She gave me a smirky, but flirty smile. "I'm a student majoring in literature and journalism at Wayne State, but I work part time as a waitress to pay tuition."

"Want to have dinner with a no-class, semi-literate, capitalistic oaf?" I gave her my best show-stopping grin.

She grinned back. "Love to. I have a great coffee house I want to show you afterwards. You like folk music—Peter, Paul, and Mary stuff?"

"Sure. Say, you look like Mary Travers." Mr. Cool knew what he was doing.

She smiled self-consciously and blushed. "Well, you *do* have a casual sophistication about you. I think you'll be all right in spite of being an engineer." She gave me a little wink.

Hot damn, casual sophistication, huh? We were off and running.

Meanwhile, after thirteen months and now on my own, the job was going along just fine until the Ford Rotunda, a Detroit landmark, burned to the ground. I was the last person from our company in the building, having visited several weeks before the disaster. I ran a test on their underground fire protection network. Everything checked out.

The fire was caused by a welder on the roof, and someone from the construction crew turned off the water supply for some reason. When I left the building, I noted in my report that the eight post indicator valves that controlled flow of water to the fire prevention system were all in the "open" position. I even put a seal with my number on each. Fire investigators noted that the seals were broken before the valves were closed. I was off the hook.

I drove to Cadillac Tower on Friday and visited with my boss, the engineer-in-charge, who reviewed my report countersigned by the Ford plant engineering manager. We were totally in the clear. The boss was still all sweaty-palmed nervous sucking down one cigarette after another.

"What are you doing tomorrow?" he wondered.

Chapter 1: The Rookie

"Driving down to see my folks. They have a family event planned; been planning it for six months."

"I think you should stay here."

"For what purpose?"

"Well, we have some executives flying in from Chicago, and they may want to talk with you."

"Fine, let's call them up and I'll talk with them now."

The boss started squirming uncomfortably, wanting to make political points. "I don't think they'll want to be bothered."

"Have they read my report?"

"Oh, yeah! Of course!"

"So what's to talk about? They'll ask me if what I wrote is true and I'll say "yes" and remind them that the Ford exec in charge of the Rotunda double-checked me and co-signed the report."

"I still think they'll want to talk with you."

"So have them call me."

"In person."

"Sorry, my family is more significant to me than some kind of clusterfuck to make Chicago feel important. If it were *really* important, I wouldn't think twice, but this—this is just pure bullshit. You know I'm right."

"Yeah, I do, but I still think you should be here just in case. If you're not, you could be making a career decision." He looked at me knowingly.

"So be it." I was not trying to be a smart ass, but had an itch to head for California and learn to surf anyway. I drove to see my parents.

The Chicago executives did come, and did want to talk with me, and did feel insulted, but I never got hammered for my political faux pas, only exposed to some half-hearted whining by my boss. That was my first exposure to the political world of business—actually a very human condition. We seem to be hard-wired to place politics above principles mostly out of fear that we will be "put out of the synagogue" or declared persona non grata. Keep in mind that I was immature and had unrealistic expectations based on youthful idealism. Sylvia was right; I didn't understand the world. I also submitted a letter of resignation. I decided that the surf was calling.

My boss called me in for a talk. "I don't want to accept this. I'd like you to fly to Chicago and talk to Maurice." Maurice, who everyone in the company pronounced "Morris," was his boss. "Well my mind is pretty much made up, but I'll be glad to talk." I figured what the hell, it's another new experience.

When I parked in the lot at Detroit Metro, a few snowflakes started falling—very few, more of a spitting. The flight was a short twenty minutes. I grabbed a cab at O'Hare and made it to the office in time for lunch.

Maurice acted like he was really glad to see me, like a long lost brother. He warmly reviewed my job performance, not sparing any superlatives. He didn't say anything about my standing up his Chicago management buddies. We went to lunch, a very pleasant and casual affair, and talked about families, sports, politics—you name it. When we went back to the office, he offered me a substantial raise to think it over. I promised I would.

I boarded the flight to Detroit about three o'clock and settled back for the short flight. As we approached Metro, the captain made an announcement.

Chapter 1: The Rookie

"Well, folks, we're here, but I need about a mile and a half visibility to land. As you can see, it's snowing out there, and we only have about a half mile. So, we'll circle awhile and see if conditions improve."

The plane was filled with murmurs of discontent. After another forty minutes of circling, the captain made another announcement.

"Well, folks, our visibility has not improved, and due to a low fuel condition, we're returning to Chicago."

The murmuring changed to loud bitching and swearing. Rats, I had a date with Sylvia and no way to contact her until we were back on the ground. However, I felt comfortable that the weather being what is was she'd figure it out.

O'Hare was total chaos. The snow storm was intense and covered an area from the Great Lakes to the Eastern Seaboard. Planes flying from the east to Cleveland, Pittsburgh, and Detroit were told to continue to Chicago. Of course, all planes that left Chicago for those destinations were instructed to return to O'Hare. Low fuel or not, we had to get into a landing queue, which burned another forty minutes, and on the ground there were not enough gates to handle the incoming hoard, so we sat on the tarmac for another three hours. Tempers were running hot. You could almost feel an urge to kill radiating from some of the passengers.

Finally, we were off the plane and gathered around an airlines representative. I called Sylvia, and received a neutral, "Yeah, whatever..." We were herded into a waiting bus, dropped at a nearby hotel, and fed. I fell asleep easily. At seven the next morning the phone rang, jogging me out of a deep sleep.

An emotionless voice said, "Be in the lobby in thirty minutes. The bus will leave for the airport whether or not you are on board."

About twelve inches of snow was on the ground, and the temperature was bone-chilling. After a ride of about thirty minutes we arrived back at O'Hare. The airline rep told us to wait while he went inside and checked flight status. We sat there awhile—how long I'm not sure because I fell asleep. The motion of the bus woke me. I asked the guy next to me what was going on. Guy said he didn't know. After exiting O'Hare, the rep got on the microphone.

"All flights from O'Hare to Detroit have been cancelled until tomorrow. The condition there is worse than here. So, we are now proceeding to the train station where we have booked you on the ten o'clock train to Detroit."

"Hey, what about our cars?" This comment was from a ruddy fellow near the front. "I'm parked at Metro."

The bus erupted with "yeahs" and "me toos."

The rep said very calmly, "You'll have to figure that out on your own."

The cacophony increased several levels with phrases like, "Son of a bitch!" and, "This is bullshit!" The rep merely sat down—end of discussion. I felt a bit sorry for him; I mean, what could he do?

After about ten minutes, the rep stood again and clicked on the audio system. We all immediately looked up expectedly.

"Folks, there is one more thing. When you get to Detroit Metro an airline representative will be expecting you. You will receive a refund for the Chicago–Detroit portion of your tickets."

There was some muted cheering accompanied by some, "Well, hell yeah!" and, "I would hope so!" comments.

Chapter 1: The Rookie

The train was not crowded, which allowed us to move freely about, plus there was a bar and dining car. Once we boarded, people started to relax. The psychological process of "acceptance" settled in, which had a calming factor. For me, it had the promise of another new adventure. We were scheduled to arrive in Detroit sometime between five and six in the evening. I considered taking the city bus from the train depot to my apartment; worry about getting my car the day after. But that's just me. I'm always trying to figure out alternative strategies while still on the move. Another option occurred to me that I liked even better. Detroit Metropolitan Airport is halfway between downtown Detroit and Ann Arbor. Why waste time traveling all the way to Detroit when I could jump off in Ann Arbor and take a taxi to Metro?

I grabbed a seat in the bar car and was joined by a road-warrior sales type guy probably in his late forties. We looked like a couple of derelicts; rumpled suits, unshaven, ties askew… actually, all the guys looked like that. The few women that were on our flight all looked surprisingly fresh. You know, one of my earliest adult observations was that ladies have some kind of magical way of pulling that off that we men will never understand.

"What're you drinkin', son?" said the sales guy, whose name was Miles. He was one of those annoying guys who add "hah-hah-hah" at the end of every sentence.

"Gin and tonic."

"Oh man, that's a ladies' drink; have something with more balls." Miles nudged me with his elbow and grinned. He looked around and hah-hah-hah chuckled knowingly to those within earshot, like he was teaching some greenhorn a lesson.

"Like what?"

"Bourbon, son. A man drinks bourbon."

"You buyin'?" The others around us were listening in, so I thought I'd put it back on him—let him play the big man. Besides, food and drink prices on trains were about three times the normal rate. Rail dining cars and bars were famous as gougers.

Miles looked around, and with a nervous little grin said, a bit too loudly, "Damn straight! (hah-hah-hah)" He elbowed me again, and winked. "Stick with me, son, and I'll have you farting through silk!" He laughed loudly at his joke, but the others only smiled to be polite.

I was still trying to recoup my losses from the Rialto Crossroads, so I looked around, and said, "Well, if we're going to be real men, shouldn't we have a beer to chase the bourbon?"

He looked at me with a forced smile. He knew he'd been had. "Sure, sure, son." And he clapped me on the back a little too hard.

When we were finished I said, "Same again on your tab?"

"Nope, nope. Got some work to do." He slumped off his stool and departed. His hah-hah-hah was somewhat forlorn.

"See you later (hah-hah-hah)," I called after him. No response.

When the train arrived in Ann Arbor about half of us decided to detrain and grab a cab for Metro. The snow was up to our knees. Six of us shared a ride that took close to an hour and a half for a normal fifteen minute ride because of road and traffic conditions. The trip was crowded and definitely uncomfortable, made more so because several decided to smoke as well.

Finally we arrived and staggered out, relieved to be free of each other. Inside the terminal, chaos abounded. People were everywhere, and the noise was incredible. There were several

Chapter 1: The Rookie

kiosks set up with beleaguered airline representatives processing tickets. We got in line for one of them and waited. By this time we were resigned to our fate. The fight had been sapped out of us. Another hour and a half and I was finally in the parking lot looking for my car. I noticed the aisles had been shoveled free of snow, but the cars were entombed. As I arrived at my car I was fortunate in that several Metro maintenance men with shovels were helping free nearby automobiles. They even had an extra shovel so I pitched in as well.

Finally in my car, I tried to start the engine. It wouldn't turn over, a victim of the cold. I was fortunate again. The maintenance crews anticipated the problem, and were able to give me a jump.

I left Metro and entered the Expressway into the absolute worst traffic jam I have ever experienced. I didn't arrive at my apartment until just before midnight, which was over four hours later.

Most of my life has been spent in Los Angeles, and I also lived in Houston eleven years. This means I am very familiar with traffic jams and tie-ups that occur on a daily basis, not that one ever gets used to it. The continual and unrelenting stop-and-go nature is so bad that a new car requires a brake job after only one year of service. That evening in Detroit produced the mother of them all.

I caught a glimpse of myself in a mirror just inside the door of my apartment. I looked like a bum; smelled like one too. I considered going to see Sylvia for comfort and physical relief, but that would mean a shower and I was too exhausted. I decided to hit the sack dirty, smelly, and with a bad case of yuck mouth. I slept through most of the next day, Sunday.

Monday morning I was completely refreshed, the streets had been cleared, and I drove to Cadillac Tower down the John Lodge Expressway for the almost the last time, singing with the radio. The song was "California Girls" by the Beach Boys. Perfect! I felt alive and free; really free.

The elevator doors opened for the thirty-eighth floor and deposited ten of us, three of whom were fellow employees, one an attractive young lady, Beth, who worked in our office. I always wanted to date her, but was too shy to ask. We knew each other only to nod "hello." I tried to make eye contact as we left the elevator, but she ignored me—again!

The office denizens looked at me strangely, not used to seeing me except on Friday. I smiled and winked at those who looked at me directly. I knew something they didn't.

Jim, the engineer-in-charge, saw me and beckoned me into his office. That's why I was there after all. He lit up a cigarette. "Coffee?" he asked, then called for Beth.

"No thanks." Beth appeared at the door. She still didn't look at me. To her I was invisible.

"Yes, Jim?" Her voice had a musical tone.

"Would you bring me a coffee, please?" he said, then looked at me, and for the first time that morning so did Beth, but she did so with a detached sense of duty. "Sure you won't have something?"

I smiled, shook my head, and winked at Beth who gave the tiniest gasp, lips parting ever so slightly. "Thanks, but no," I said still making eye contact with Beth.

She blushed and left. Jim was oblivious to the whole dynamic.

"Well, I understand you had a nice visit with Maurice," he began benevolently.

"Yes, it was quite nice." Beth brought the coffee trying not to look at me, but I caught her giving me a bit of a sideways glance—just enough to be encouraging.

Chapter 1: The Rookie

Jim sipped his coffee, took a drag on his cigarette, and sat back blowing smoke at the ceiling. "How was the rest of the trip?"

Was he kidding? Had he not watched weather reports on television? Had he not heard the nonstop patter on the radio of airports closed all over the Midwest?

"Terrible; the worst trip in the entire human history of trips," I said easily, then leaned forward and gave him the details. I ended the narrative with, "Maurice and all of you have been great, and I've enjoyed working for you, but my resignation at the end of the year stands. Thanks for all you've taught me. Besides after that Rotunda business… well, you know. Sooner or later it'll come back to bite me in the ass."

"Nah, memories are short." He stabbed out his cigarette.

"I also think the journey back from Chicago was an omen; time for me to get out of Dodge."

"You know, that doesn't make a whole hell of a lot of sense, but I understand." He lit up another smoke. "What are you going to do?"

"I'm moving to California."

He gave me this abbreviated snort, the "you stupid kid" kind. "You have a job?"

"Not yet, but I wrote to Carnation in L.A. about an opening in their plant engineering department. I have an interview with them as soon as I get there."

He sighed. "Well, fine. You'll still be here for our office Christmas party this Friday; we'll have a drink together then, okay?"

"Sure, and thanks again, Jim." I rose and we shook hands.

On the way out, I walked by Beth's desk, gave her a smile, and casually said, "See you."

This time she smiled back. I cursed myself for waiting so long. Now it was too late. Once outside, I laughed to myself, relieved at the sense of closure I felt along with the electric excitement of an anticipated new beginning in California.

The office party was one hell of a lot of fun. They always were back in the day when booze and sex flowed freely without the interference of tort lawyers always looking for someone to sue. I received congratulations from almost everyone about my plans to move west. During the preceding week I made plans to drive there with a friend two days after Christmas. I was into my third cocktail when a well endowed forty-something lady—today we call them cougars—pulled me into the lavish corner office and closed the door. Her ample cleavage pinned me to the nearest wall. I enjoyed the sensation, but hadn't consumed enough on liquor to feel at ease. I was a bit frightened.

"You know whose office this is?" purred the cougar.

"Yeah, it's Andy's, the big guy; the manager-in-charge," I said losing myself in her eyes while smelling liquor on her breath mixed with an exotic perfume.

"Right," she smiled, kissing me. "It's my husband's."

She stuck her thigh between my legs. "What if he comes in?" I gasped.

"Don't worry; he won't be here for another hour." She started massaging and kissing me.

I was getting braver by the minute, but I didn't want to cuckold Andy, him being such a nice guy, and anyway there's the "guy rule" about not screwing your friends' girls. Of course, Andy really wasn't my friend.... Maybe being your

Chapter 1: The Rookie

boss's boss doesn't count, I thought, looking for a loophole. "What if someone comes in?"

"You worry too much, little man. The lights are off and the door is locked. We are quite alone. Nobody's going to save you." She shoved me down on the couch.

I'm pretty sure I got raped, but must admit it was a wonderful experience, and one I relived for years. Thirty minutes later I was out with the rest of the cheerful crowd absolutely full of euphoria. I spotted Beth with some of the other girls and decided to go chat her up. I was bubbling with confidence, partly from the booze and partly from getting laid.

She grinned broadly as I approached. "Hi," she said. "I thought you were never going to talk to me. Where have you been?"

"Oh, just out by the elevator talking to some of the guys."

"I heard you're leaving next week."

I nodded. "Yeah, going to head west."

"So why haven't you tried to date me?"

I couldn't tell her I was frightened so I told her a half-truth. "You never seemed interested; never even looked at me. I didn't think you even knew I existed, but to save my ego I told myself you had a boyfriend."

She laughed. "Oh, my God!" Then she took my hand, noticing that I was taken aback by her reaction. "Wanna take me home?"

Why, oh why did I wait so long? Beth was terrific, but now it was too late. On the other hand, it was a good thing. I may have never left.

Chapter 2

Guaymas

I LEFT gray, dreary Detroit for the promise of sunny southern California with my best friend, Dennis, two days after Christmas. We packed his Triumph TR-3 roadster to the hilt and headed west. The trip took an unhurried four days, marred only by a minor mechanical breakdown in Albuquerque. Mostly it was relaxing and uneventful.

After arriving in the Los Angeles area and taking a week to get settled, I called Carnation to arrange for the interview they promised before I left Detroit. The office was on Wilshire Boulevard, which fueled my already high expectations. It turned out to be a huge letdown. Their factories were located all over the US, all in *very* out-of-the-way places—like South Dakota. The job was to provide engineering support on a rotating basis to all of these plants. The interviewer informed me I would be away from Los Angeles for six months at a time. This was bad news for a youngster who wanted to live in the beach community and learn to surf.

Chapter 2: Guaymas

I could hear the voices of my former boss in Detroit and my parents in sing-song voices harmonizing, "Nyah-nyah, nyah-nyah-nyah; I told you so!"

Fortunately, engineering employment opportunities abounded, so a quick canvassing of the want ads resulted in plenty of job interviews. Within a month, I was hired by a Fortune 500 manufacturer of gas-fired heating and control systems. Better yet, the factory was located near the beach area. My job was to perform various tests within the engineering laboratory, much of which was research and development. Many of the engineers were young and single, like me, and I made friends easily. We played in industrial softball and basketball leagues, attended Dodger and Angel games every week, went deep sea fishing, flew to Las Vegas in the middle of the week for all night gambling, and frequented the beach area lounges looking for ladies. Life was good. Then I got promoted.

Where before I just wanted to put in my hours—and I did so with pride in my work—then go horse around with the boys, after the promotion I became ambitious and a bit full of myself. I decided I wanted to big a big shot executive; be looked upon as someone exceptional, and live on the hill in Palos Verdes. Over the ensuing three years, most of my friends moved to other jobs, and I fell under the influence of a new engineering executive, relocated from corporate headquarters, to spearhead a new product. He chose me for his team, and I felt fortunate. My group was to perform rigorous tests on the new product and approve it for production. Little did I know it was fraught with serious technical and legal problems and would cost me weekends, holidays, and vacations. It also cost me my career with the company, which will become clear later in this narrative.

Looking back, it was amazing to learn how one's ambition can blind him from reality. Take the new, big cheese, engineering executive, John, for instance. Years later, I could see the guy was a nut, but at the time it was my plan to ride his coattails to the top. One evening late after work, he decided to take a few of us to an expensive restaurant in Redondo Beach for cocktails, steak, and fine wine. He liked to do that—play the role.

When the waiter brought the salads, John demanded frozen forks—and got them.

The waiter asked if we wanted ground pepper, but before he could apply it, John said,

"Wait, let me check it first." He twisted the handle and exclaimed, "Aha, just as I thought! I *must* adjust the grind. Waiter, bring me a small crescent wrench!" The best that could be found was a pair of pliers. John adjusted the little nut on the bottom until the cracked pepper was the size he preferred. I admit that his arrogance made the rest of us uncomfortable, but ambition can blind one.

Just before the steaks, a bottle of Pinot Noir arrived. Uh-oh, I thought. Uh-oh was right. John took a small sip and said, "Hmmm, sixty-five degrees. It should be fifty-four. Waiter, this must be eleven degrees cooler!" The guy brought an ice bucket to the table, and twisted the bottle in it for about three minutes, and offered it to John again.

"Almost. It's fifty-seven degrees."

The waiter was sweating bullets before John finally approved.

Much to my surprise, the steaks and dessert met with John's immediate approval. I suppose by then, he decided he had been "impressive" enough, but it's just as likely that he was simply hungry. Finally, the waiter dropped off the bill, and John said to us,

"Watch and learn." He wrote his name and address, Palos Verdes of course, on the check and ordered us to get up and

Chapter 2: Guaymas

leave. As we walked out the door, the waiter came running out in a state of panic waving the tab. John took the poor guy aside and talked him into mailing the bill!

As we were about to part in the parking lot John lit up his pipe, got this big shit-eating grin on his face and declared, "I'll be a bit late tomorrow. The IRS called me in about my federal return."

"I'll bet you're really nervous. I would be," I said.

"Are you kidding? I love dueling with those incompetent clowns. I claim everything under the moon—I mean—I really get ridiculous! I'll negotiate, and they'll cut half of it, which is still twice as much as I deserve. I love it. It's my favorite time of year."

Another time I went with him to the airport to pick up one of his corporate colleagues. John pulled right into the loading zone with his big, expensive automobile, parked, locked the doors, and went inside, me trailing behind. A public address systems announced in a continual loop. "The white zone is for loading and unloading of passengers only. No parking!"

"Hey, John, your car will be towed," I said, a bit panicky.

He looked at me, grinned, and sighed. "Your car they would tow. When you have a car like mine, you can park wherever you wish." He looked back and waved at his car. "They never tow these kinds of cars." With that he sniffed, took a drag on his pipe, and walked ahead with his nose in the air.

I felt myself wishing his car would be towed. It wasn't.

Meanwhile, I continued to do John's bidding at work, making my whole group put in late hours to make up for design and model shop schedule slips. When we discovered unfavorable results, we were told to retest or ignore the data for the greater good of the company. The product, though a marketer's dream, was plagued with fatal flaws, some of which could compromise safety. With gas controlled systems, property and lives are at stake. Finally, ambition or not, my group decided to kill the product. Our final report said that approval to continue was not granted by the test engineering department. We listed a long series of problems along with corrective recommendations. That was not good news to management. John and a host of executives were livid. The product went to production without approval. I was no longer popular.

Less than a year later, the *Wall Street Journal* ran an article about safety risks of the product. Problems—serious problems—had occurred. Property had been damaged. Lives had not been lost, but according to the article, that was just a matter of time. Tort lawyers were lining up. My group's files were purged, meaning all of our data books and reports were rounded up and destroyed. I was reassigned to the other side of the factory. The company worked around the clock redesigning and replacing the product with one that looked similar, but did not contain all of the "new marketing benefits." The careers of anyone involved, including John's and mine, were over.

As I sat in my office one day working on my resume and confirming job interviews, the telephone rang. On the other end was my brother, Jim, who worked in San Diego for an aerospace company.

"What are you doing next week?" he asked.

"Looking for a job." I told him the story.

"Listen, I've got just the thing for you—something to get rid of the stress; get you out of that toilet. Interested?"

"Man, am I! Anything to get my life restarted. What d'ya got?"

Chapter 2: Guaymas

"Basketball in Mexico." He paused to let it sink in. "Five days in Guaymas drinking too much, getting some sun and salt water on our bods, and playing hoops."

He explained the details of a Mexican tournament his industrial league team in San Diego had entered, but some of the guys' wives wouldn't let them go; they were short players—really short. Of the twelve team members, only six could go, and they were required by tournament rules to have a minimum of seven. Jim and his teammates played Division I college basketball for teams like Michigan, Stanford, and USC. I was a high school scrub, still playing in an inferior industrial league, which shows just how desperate they were.

I didn't think twice. "I'm in." Then I called my boss to tell him I was taking a week of personal time. Another nail in my career coffin, but I was history either way.

The following week I drove to San Diego to rendezvous with the rest of the team. We gathered at the team captain's—a guy named Dutton—place in El Centro for the drive to Mexicali, and a train ride to Guaymas. Three of the guys—Dutton, Baker, and Schultz—brought their wives, making our group a round number of ten. Dutton's twelve-passenger van was our transportation to the train station. We piled in and the journey began.

Dutton was a block of a guy built more like an NFL linebacker than a basketball player. He possessed a cheerful, apple-checked face, and a sunny disposition. To him, there was no middle ground in anything, only extremes. You know the type… drink a gallon of milk or no milk; eat everything in sight or eat nothing. He drove the same way—the accelerator all the way on the floor, or all the way off the floor. Needless to say, it was a harrowing ride, complete with beer drinking and loud belching. The ladies also participated. Amazingly, we arrived unharmed at the train station in Mexicali.

Boarding the train was uneventful, but the coaches were ancient without a pretense of comfort. The seventeen-hour ride on hard seats was challenging, but at least occupancy was light and afforded us plenty of room to spread out. As we settled in, a vendor came through selling beer and sandwiches. Dutton made sure we had all the beer and sandwiches we could handle over the next three hours.

Everyone in our small group was familiar with each other, save me. I was the only new face, and at thirty-seven, also the oldest. I suggested to the others that we keep in mind that we were in a foreign country as guests and conduct ourselves accordingly. The idea was to keep a low profile and not provide any stereotypical Ugly American material. That made sense to everyone but the remaining two of our group, Carlos and Reuben, both Mexican nationals. In their youthful exuberance, they loudly dribbled basketballs from one end of the train to the other while laughing, jostling, and playing grab-ass, much to the irritation of the other passengers. I saw keeping those two in check would be unlikely. Reuben was of lesser concern because he "looked Mexican" and would be pegged as such by his countrymen.

Carlos was another matter entirely. He was blond-haired, blue-eyed, and looked like a six-nine southern California surfer. He even sounded like one, using the beach dialect liberally with no hint of a Spanish accent. Carlos was reputed to be the finest raw basketball talent to come from the San Diego area, and that included Bill Walton. Another reputation dogged him: head case. The *Los Angeles Times* reported he was losing his scholarship at USC and enrolling at Long Beach State, a haven for troubled players.

About 9:00 the next morning, the train stopped in the middle of the Sonora Desert at a small town called Benjamin Hill. We took our belongings, disembarked, and waited for the train to Guaymas, which was scheduled to arrive two hours

Chapter 2: Guaymas

later. None of us was able to catch much sleep, so we haunted the hot, dusty streets like zombies with beer breath. Benjamin Hill looked like one of those old-time, cowboy-movie western towns—complete with rolling tumbleweeds. Saguaro cacti surrounded the place, silently standing guard. For breakfast, I purchased three tamales from some lady selling in the street, and washed them down with freshly squeezed orange juice. A bit later, Baker found a cantina that was open, so we spent the rest of our waiting time drinking Mexican beer and eating fresh tortillas. Carta Blanca—breakfast of champions. Now that's a training table, sports fans.

Shortly after 11:00, we boarded the connecting train to Guaymas—on our way again. Dutton procured quesadillas and beer for lunch from an on-train vendor. The quesadillas were unlike any I'd ever seen; a nine-inch round of some kind of white cheese, which were not sandwiched between two tortillas—just cheese. Whatever, they were tasty enough.

Reuben and Carlos continued to annoy the rest of the passengers with their horseplay and tone of voice to the conductor and vendors, which was overly gruff and demanding. I had no idea what the two were saying, but it riled most of the others causing them to quickly abandon the coach in which we were riding. The boys seemed to get a kick out of running people off. Finally, at 3:40 Friday afternoon the train pulled into the station at Guaymas. We arrived a little more than three hours before the tip-off of our first game. What a team—half drunk and going on almost no sleep.

Our first reaction to the city of Guaymas was stunned and delighted amazement. Our spirits and energy picked up immediately. The town was in the midst of a colorful and noisy festival that was to continue for the entire weekend. In addition to the basketball tournament, racing events were scheduled for bicycling and water skiing. The former had about one-thousand entries from all over North America, and the latter thirty participants, mostly from Arizona. What a fiesta! Our chances for maintaining some sort of focus on basketball, and remaining sober enough to play well looked slim.

At first inspection, the eight-team basketball tournament draw seemed pretty mundane. Nothing to worry about. Play a few games, maybe win a few (or not), drink some beer, and have a good time. One bracket consisted of Hermosillo, La Paz, Obregon, and Mexicali (us). The other bracket included Guaymas, the host and tournament favorite (I'll get to that later), along with Ciudad Juarez, Puerto Vallarta, and Mazatlan. Although the tourney was single elimination, each team got to play at least two games, because the first game losers would play preliminary games for the first game winners on Saturday. The championship game was scheduled for eleven o'clock Sunday morning. By then, we expected to be doing nothing but enjoying the fiesta.

Then Dutton received the roster for the other teams.

Largely unknown in the US is that Mexico has very good semi-pro basketball leagues, especially in the State of Sonora. At that time, the composition of the teams in those leagues consisted largely of ex-college athletes from the US, and some excellent Mexican players. During the long train ride through the Sonora Desert, I was astonished to see more outside basketball courts than baseball and soccer fields combined. Anyway, guess who made up the rosters for the other teams in the tournament? Hint: It wasn't industrial league stiffs like us.

The information Dutton received about whom we would be competing against psychologically caused us to reconsider our cavalier attitudes. Fun, though our *raison d'etre*, was no longer our primary concern. We could handle losing, but didn't want to be outright embarrassed. The situation looked bleak. Then again, we thought maybe our first opponent, Hermosillo, wouldn't be that good. That turned out to be a faulty assumption.

Chapter 2: Guaymas

The top seed was the host team, Guaymas, which in reality was the University of New Mexico bolstered by several young coaches, recently graduated, that also played. The second seed was our first opponent. The Mexican Olympic Team, fresh off a fourth place finish in the Montreal Olympics, represented Hermosillo. We suddenly felt very tired; embarrassment seemed certain.

The arena was quite nice. The playing surface was larger than those of the US being the standard International size. There was only one problem, and it was major. The laminated wood playing surface was bordered with beautifully polished tiles. It was like stepping on an ice rink when you left the floor boundaries, something that happens frequently during the course of a game, especially when driving to the basket. I mean, it was aesthetically pleasing, but dangerous as hell. Other than that, everything about the venue was first rate. The stands were packed with rabid, Mexican basketball fans. Many had been there most of the day, having attended the afternoon games. Now they settled in to enjoy the two main events featuring second seeded Hermosillo, in the first evening game, and the favored host team in the second. The atmosphere was electric and festive.

We arrived early enough to observe the second half of the La Paz versus Obregon contest, and were impressed by the skill and conditioning of both teams. Obregon made up an eight point deficit with a flurry of accurate outside shots, and won the game in the last two minutes. The winner of our game (Hermosillo versus Mexicali) would face Obregon the following afternoon.

At least we "stood out" aesthetically. All other teams had snazzy uniforms with the names of their cities on the front. Our uniforms were tattered, old, and faded with Jules Liquor Store gaudily splashed across them. When we took the floor, Carlos, egged on by Reuben, started taunting some of the fans, especially when he threw down some thundering slam-dunks during warm-up drills. Just what we need, I thought. In addition to being exhausted, a bit boozy, and playing the Mexican Olympic Team, why not irritate the fans as well? International referees—I don't care what country—have the reputation of being influenced by the home crowd. We were already worried Carlos would mouth off when called for a foul, and get thrown out. If that happened, a one-sided drubbing for sure would be our embarrassing fate. Well, I thought I might be able to do something about that. I had an idea that was hatched by some information I learned on the train.

When we initially entered the arena, I was introduced to the tournament director; an upbeat, energetic guy named Manual, who ran a tight ship. He insisted everyone call him Manny. I immediately liked him. During pre-game warm-ups, I saw Manny standing near the scorer's table. I left the drills and approached him.

"Hey, amigo, how's it going for you?" he asked with a grin and a wink as I neared. He also pumped my hand enthusiastically.

"Well, we're pretty tired, and that's a very good team we have to play," I said rolling my eyes.

"Si, they are *very* good. I hope you can give them a game so I won't lose the crowd before Guaymas plays." Manny's eyes actually twinkled.

I think what he meant is that he hoped we wouldn't get laughed off the floor. Everyone would undoubtedly remain for the "home" team. They'd also enjoy watching their Olympians beat up on a bunch of gringos. Time for my great idea.

"You know, I'm not sure you're aware of this," I began seriously, "but see that big, blond kid on our team? Number twenty-four?"

Chapter 2: Guaymas

"Si, I see him. He acts poquito loco, no?"

"Oh, no, no. He's just fooling around… having some fun," I said, waving my hand back and forth. "Anyway, he's a member of the Mexican National Team that will be playing in the World University Games in Moscow next month."

"Really?" said Manny, clearly surprised.

"Yeah. Maybe it might be a good idea during the introductions to let the crowd know who he is. You know, one of their own." I looked at him hopefully.

"May-bee…." Manny shrugged.

When our team was introduced, Carlos was referred to only as a player from the University of Southern California. The crowd whistled derisively, which they continued to do every time each touched the ball. Carlos responded with obscene gestures. Great, I thought.

The game started on a very bizarre note, which was fortunate for us. The Hermosillo team, perhaps taking our ragtag team lightly, began the game remarkably flat and lethargic, while we had a surprising amount of energy and hit everything we threw in the direction of our goal. In particular, Brother Jim, Baker, and Carlos couldn't miss. I played only three minutes, and mainly tried to stay out of the way. By halftime, we had a surprising eighteen point lead. Frustrated, the crowd directed their animosity toward Hermosillo because of the inept first half performance of the Olympians, which took the heat off Carlos. On the downside, Carlos received one technical foul for his constant whining, and was warned by the referees that unless he controlled his mouth, he would be ejected. In addition, when Carlos thought he had been wronged, he would just stand and glare at the officials while the game continued. This created a huge defensive liability, and I understood why the USC coaching staff gave up on him.

When the second half began, Hermosillo came out fired up and focused; and the long train ride, beer, and lack of sleep finally caught up with us. Hermosillo applied tremendous defensive pressure, making it difficult for us to score, and ran a lethal fast break every time they got a defensive rebound, which resulted in many easy baskets. We were gasping to keep up. But in the end, through good fortune—Hermosillo missed several easy shots in the last minute of play—we withstood their furious rally and held on for a two-point upset. The crowd was stunned. So was Hermosillo. So were we.

In the second game, Guaymas blew out Mazatlan by twenty-two points, led by a talented, rough-and-tumble center named Ward. He owned the inside; a man against boys. They looked unbeatable.

We were so giddy from our unexpected win that we joined the festival downtown, eating and drinking until the wee hours of the morning. Some of the Arizona water ski racing people were largely responsible for our late hours. They enjoyed the game and wanted to hang out with us, which included purchasing numerous rounds of adult beverages. I couldn't help but wonder if the racers were prudent staying out and drinking so much. Their first heats began the next morning, and since they skied at speeds exceeding one-hundred mile per hour, I assumed they prefer to race cold sober and well rested. Turned out my assumption was faulty.

We awoke in a fog between ten and eleven the next morning. The day was glorious and warm. It was ninety degrees, but didn't feel hot. It felt perfect. Jim and I went for a run to flush out our lungs. When we returned, Dutton met us. He was beaming.

"Check it out," he said pointing to his left. One by one the others began to emerge from their rooms squinting, yawning, scratching, and stretching. There in a parking spot in front of his motel room sat a Volkswagen Jeep-like contraption. At that

Chapter 2: Guaymas

time it was called the Thing but later renamed Safari. Dutton had removed the top and side curtains.

"I rented us a team bus," he said, looking around for approval. "We beat maybe the best team in the tournament," and added with a wink, "Which may also be our last win." Everyone nodded and grinned. "Because of that monumental accomplishment, I figure we deserve better transportation than the city bus system."

"Yeah.... but there are ten of us," said Jim. "Where will we all fit?"

"Shit, man, we just all climb in and hang on best we can. What do you say we head for the beach?"

Baker looked concerned, and gave Dutton a sideways look. "You drivin'?"

Somehow we all squeezed in, Reuben and Carlos sitting on the front fenders. The poor, overloaded vehicle was riding on the rear axle. Dutton floored the accelerator and ground the gears speed-shifting into second.

"El Segundo!" everyone yelled.

Our first stop was to pick up two bottles of Sauza, my favorite Tequila, a case of beer, and a case of Cokes. The people of Guaymas gawked at the strange vehicle filled with seven men and three women. Whenever we stopped, young boys surrounded Jim, Baker, and Carlos and asked how tall each was, followed by a dozen other questions in rapid succession. This scene played out time after time during our stay.

The beach was exquisite with fine white sand and the bluest water I'd ever seen. The clear sky closely matched the color of the water. Huge rocks, like great, rounded pyramids, popped out of the ocean forty meters or so offshore, and contrasted with the Saguaro on the hills overlooking the beach. The desert literally met the sea.

As we lolled in waist-deep water passing a bottle back and forth, an occasional mullet leapt into the air, sometimes not more than several feet away. The sight of the fish combined with the tequila and no breakfast made us aware of our hunger. Luckily, Dutton spied a young boy on the beach attempting to sell something contained in a large stainless steel pot. We descended on the lad like locusts. The pot was full of tamales, maybe fifty. We bought them all and consumed every one, washing them down with great swigs of beer. Refreshed and sated, we jumped back on our "bus" and headed downtown for some more merriment.

Our stay in town was short since we faced Obregon in the second afternoon game scheduled to tip-off at four o'clock. We were pretty optimistic about our chances until Reuben twisted his ankle screwing around with Carlos. Jim gave the young Mexican a thorough taping job, which we hoped would be effective. Fortunately, it was. I mean, the other option was for me to get a lot of playing time, which wouldn't bode well for our chance at victory.

We arrived in time to see the end of the first game. The disappointing Hermosillo team played like the Olympians they were, and easily dispatched an outmanned La Paz team, but the slick tiles claimed one of their players. It was a good thing we didn't have to play them that day. We wouldn't have stood much of a chance. Just before the game ended, I saw my new friend, Manny the tournament director, so I walked over and made a second petition on behalf of Carlos.

He looked at me vacantly, and smiled with his mouth, but not his eyes. The unspoken communication was that we screwed up his tournament. "I think Mexicali was very fortunate last night, no?" Manny shook his head from frustration.

"Very fortunate," I agreed.

Chapter 2: Guaymas

"Well, it should not be so difficult with Obregon," Manny sighed drifting over to an official trying to get his attention. "Play well, amigo." Then he was gone.

Rats, I thought. Foiled again.

Led by the scoring of our big front line, and some excellent all around floor play by Reuben—in relief of Dutton and Schultz—we beat Obregon handily. Carlos continued to irritate the fans and the referees; and I played about four minutes each half, passing the ball as soon as I got it, and tried to play some semblance of cagey veteran clutch-and-grab defense. In spite of Carlos' attitude and my ineptness, we made it to the championship final.

"Hey, Dutton," I said. "Think we ought to come back and scout the Guaymas game tonight? There's no way they won't be our opponent tomorrow morning. They have a lock."

"What for?" he asked with amusement. "What are we going to learn watching them blow out Puerto Vallarta? Anyway, it's a fiesta, man! Time to enjoy!"

I had to admit he had a point.

We piled back on the Thing and headed downtown, still wearing our ratty basketball uniforms. Dutton ground second gear with every shift drawing shouts of "El Segundo!" from the rest of us. I have little recollection of the rest of that afternoon and the night, except for eating a chicken tamale with a whole chicken wing in it, bone and all, about three in the morning. I also vaguely recall running into some of the Guaymas players somewhere, and drinking beer with them.

Nancy Baker pounded on my door about ten the next morning. "Hey, get the hell up! We got a game in an hour!"

My head was pounding. "Wha...." I moaned through the closed door.

"I mean it, get your ass out of bed and help me get the others up!" She sounded very annoyed. Her husband gave me an "out of it" goofy grin when I peeked through the front curtains.

"Ohhh...." I groaned when the sunlight streamed in.

The previous night's activity didn't affect Dutton's driving technique, and in some way, I think the nerve-racking trip and fresh morning air did us some good. It certainly woke us up. A half dozen "El Segundos" later, we arrived at the arena twenty minutes prior to tip-off; just in time to get a short warm-up. Guaymas was already halfway through their drills when we walked into the packed and noisy arena, but I couldn't help but notice they looked a little green around the gills as well. I thought maybe we wouldn't get clobbered too badly after all.

The first ten minutes of the game confirmed my theory. Both teams were sluggish, and plodded up and down the floor it what seemed like slow motion. I caught Schultz's eye from my seat on the bench as he trotted past me to the defensive end of the floor. "Looks like the Hangover Championship of North America!" I called.

"Feels like it too!" he yelled back.

Guaymas consistently maintained a four to six point lead during the early stages. In our favor, we seemed to be recovering better than they were, and Carlos was having a superb game while staying in control of his emotions. We found the key—alcohol. In their favor was Truman Ward, the big center. He was too strong for any of our big men, who couldn't keep him from scoring inside and rebounding almost at will. I later found out he was a non-drinker. Still, we weren't embarrassed, and were content with the score as close as it was. We had no illusions of winning the game—just didn't want to look bad.

Our young opponents started the second half with a spurt, and with Ward leading the way, increased their lead to twelve points with just eight minutes to play. I got into the game for about two minutes, just long enough to get a rebound, and get knocked on my can by their big center. When I returned to the bench, I called a timeout. (Note: In international rules, all timeouts must be called from the bench.)

"What'd you do that for?" asked Schultz coming off the floor with our confused teammates.

"I dunno. Thought maybe you could use an extra blow," I said vacantly. "Hell, we have three timeouts left, and we can't take them with us. Might as well use them. Maybe we can think of something to keep them from turning this into a complete runaway."

"I think Baker and I already have," said Jim.

"Yeah," said Baker. "Let's post up Dutton, and also let Dutton wrestle with Ward on defense. None of us (pointing to himself, Jim, and Carlos) can keep him away from the basket."

"Sounds okay to me," Dutton shrugged. "Ain't nothin' to lose."

I need to pause in my narrative to mention several key points about this strategy. I mentioned earlier that Dutton was a bit of a brute. Our big guys mentioned that they couldn't move whenever he leaned on them in pick-up games. Even though he gave up four inches to Ward, Jim and Baker believed he could take Ward out of the game as a scorer and rebounder. Another point had to do with the consistency of the referees. They called a good game, but apparently believed there was no such thing as a charging foul. By putting Dutton, a guard, in the low post and feeding the ball to him, he could turn into and literally steamroller the smaller guard assigned to him. This would accomplish four things: 1) stop Ward, 2) get us some easy baskets, 3) foul out their guards, and 4) stop the clock by getting free throw attempts. If Ward decided to pick Dutton up, Dutton could feed the ball to Jim, Baker, or Carlos, all with deadly accuracy.

The strategy worked well, but with about five and a half minutes left, we were still down by eight points. Then we received some unexpected help. Dutton's offensive tactics infuriated Guaymas, especially when he gave one of them a bloody nose, and the recipient was called for a foul. They stopped playing and began complaining. It took them out of their game—just enough. Dutton continued to score points and dispense bruises on offense, and shut down Ward on defense. We crept within one point. With nine seconds left, Jim hit a jumper from the corner, which gave us our first and only lead of the contest. Baker intercepted the Guaymas inbound pass at mid-court, and the game was over. Everyone was stunned: the crowd, our opponents, and most of all, us.

During the trophy presentation, Manny finally made the announcement I begged him of a few days earlier. The crowd was momentarily shocked, then gave a tearful Carlos a rousing ovation. In addition, with twenty-four points, Carlos was selected as the MVP of the game. More cheers brought more tears from Carlos.

We left the arena for the last time, squeezed into and unto the Thing, and went downtown again in our uniforms for (what else?) tamales and beer.

That was the glorious end of my undistinguished basketball career. It was the last time I played organized ball. During our short time together, I felt a special and unusual closeness to that group of people. It was a unique feeling—a once in a lifetime feeling.

Other than Jim, I never saw any of them again.

Chapter 3

Around the World in Forty Days

I DECIDED to write this narrative like it's happening in the moment. It seems more exciting that way, and I am, after all, rather quirky.

Part 1: Aberdeen

So here I am scrunched into seat 35C under a blanket that I'm holding up like a tent. Somewhere inside the massive fuselage of a British Airways 747, cruising at an altitude of forty-one thousand feet, moisture has condensed, traveled a random path, and found an inconvenient escape right over my head. The first unexpected baptism soaked my shirt with a brown, greasy stain, and the deluge has continued at certain, but unpredictable intervals. Under my breath I mutter curses that I booked the flight after all seats were sold in business and first classes.

Chapter 3: Around the World in Forty Days

It's middle of the night, middle of the Atlantic, every seat covered with sweating crotches and alien buttocks of all sizes and shapes, most emitting regular eruptions of flatulence, some audible, but most of the hissing church-type variety. Added to this barnyard ambience is a bouquet of BO and halitosis spewing forth amid saliva bubbles from slumbering human forms. If we must spend a third of our lives in an unconscious state, why does it have to look and smell like this? I figure God must get a kick out of assigning us ludicrous attributes for the benefit of his own amusement. I can just see Him standing by a monitor, and yelling to the heavenly hosts, "Hey, you guys! C'mere quick! Check out this one!" Think I'm kidding? Tell you what: put a mirror in front of your face during your next orgasm.

A wandering, bored flight attendant noticing my distress offhandedly clucks that "it" should stop soon.

"What, the Chinese water torture or the farts?" Not only am I a smart aleck, but an irritated smart aleck.

She pretends not to hear me. Philistine!

Hours later, I stagger off the aircraft, sleep deprived, soiled shirt, into the frenetic pace of Gatwick morning (about 6:00 a.m.), and mosey toward the domestic departure concourse. After a bleary-eyed wait of indeterminate time, I somehow manage to board a plane—to this day I don't remember doing it—that arrives in Aberdeen, Scotland about 9:15. Everything in Aberdeen is gray (grey if you're a Brit) houses, stores, commercial buildings, the weather—everything! The most abundant building material is gray granite, and the most abundant weather, courtesy of the North Sea, is gray fog. At least there is some semblance of order. I like that.

A short taxi ride later and I'm checking into a picturesque Scottish inn called the Trees. My appointment is for 1:00 p.m., so upon checking in, I down a shot of brandy offered by the desk clerk—the other choice is sherry—very civilized of them to my way of thinking; and attempt to catch an hour or two under a Lone Ranger type sleep mask given to me by the airlines. Mostly I just lie there—and rip 'em off. Real window rattlers. And no one around to receive the benefit of my efforts! Wish I'd had some of that ammo to combat my fellow 747 passengers.

Damned if soon as I get to my appointment, a factory that sells and services oil-drilling tools, I don't run into this field engineer from Lafayette, Louisiana, a real coon-ass known as Kufu. His real name is James something-or-other. Nobody knows for sure.

Kufu is a legend in the oil patch, a good engineer to be sure, but also a real character, which is saying something if you've ever been involved with an industry full of characters. Once on the way to Bossier City, I stopped by his office in Lafayette. Said he was heading my way to meet customers, and would I like to fly along with him in his private airplane. I mentioned that his ratty-looking tennis shoes, most in the oil patch wear boots, seemed a bit inappropriate. Kufu looked at them, sighed, and agreed. He also pulled a can of white spray paint from his bottom drawer, and painted the shoes, while still on his feet, and some of the carpet as well.

Another time he invited certain company big-cheeses, including his CEO, and some customers to his little shotgun house on a bayou for a crayfish boil. Or as his diminutive (five feet three inches), unkempt self put it, in coon-ass-ese and gravely voice, "We go lake, have ba-ba-ku."

Well, it got a bit crowded, in fact a whole lot crowded. No problem. Kufu fired up a chainsaw and took out a wall, electrical wiring and all.

Last time on the way to Aberdeen, three of us, including Kufu, had to make a stop in Iceland to check out some geothermal drilling activity. Night before our early morning flight

Chapter 3: Around the World in Forty Days

to the UK, Kufu made the acquaintance of a local couple and went off somewhere with them. Later we found out that the guy wanted to watch while Kufu screwed his wife.

As we're leaving the hotel before sunrise and walk by Kufu's room, we find the door wide open with Kufu bare-assed naked on his bed passed out like a stone. Big piss hard-on standing up like a flagstaff. Our sleeping beauty wouldn't stir so we left him to catch the next flight, which departed two days later—give him extra time with voyeur and wife. For the entertainment of other hotel guests we did not close his door.

Anyway, now having Kufu in Aberdeen with me, I resign myself to a late, sleep-deprived evening featuring the massive consumption of beer. Thankfully, that did not happen.

Turns out the local managing director, Bill Aitken, rented a Cessna so Kufu could take some aerial photographs of the factory. Now anyone who knows Kufu would know that was a really bad idea. The night before, Kufu meets two Scottish lassies in a pub and invites them to join him for the flight, providing they bring the beer. They do.

So, they're having a merry old time up there. Kufu takes some great shots, the day being clear in that pristine, fresh, autumn way, and he's getting hummers and hand-jobs from the lassies. Well, between the beer and an orgasm, Kufu becomes lost; hasn't a clue about how to return to the airport. His passengers are helpful since they know the local street layout, though unfortunately, not from an altitude of more than two meters. No worries though because Kufu gets an idea; one advanced to the front of his coon-ass brain by beer and a semen release. He puts the Cessna into a dive, and flies close enough to the deck for the lassies to read the street signs. This strategy works like a charm. He's taxiing to the hangar in no time. Too bad the British version of FAA is waiting for him.

I heard later that Aitken's company received one hell of a fine. Not sure how long Kufu was delayed, but I never saw him over the two days I remained.

Part 2: Netherlands

The flight to Amsterdam is brief, and I board the train for Bergen right there at Schipol Airport. Bergen is an idyllic, seaside artist's colony located about half an hour out of Amsterdam. I check into a quaint inn in the middle of the quaint town, and walk the quaint main drag in search of a quaint pub. This place is really fucking quaint. According to the signs posted in the windows of most storefronts, this is a good weekend to be in Bergen. A jazz concert and sailing regatta are scheduled for the next three days. Action will abound!

I hadn't stepped more than ten meters from the inn when two six-year old, toe-headed hooligans sporting toy wooden guns confront me.

"Halt," they command in unison.

I figure I'll play along.

"*Geuje middag*," I say, putting my hands on my head.

"*Dag, maneer*," the leader acknowledges. Then in English, "You will give me your papers!" He tries to say this with a menacing face, but his visage is just too cherubic.

I hand over my passport.

After a few moments of concentrated, brow-furrowed, head-knotted scrutiny, the little guy says,

"Your papers are in order. You may pass."

"*Dank u well*," I say bowing slightly.

"*Austoblift*," they answer together.

I hadn't taken two or three steps, when I hear...

Chapter 3: Around the World in Forty Days

"Halt!"

I turn and stare into two very grave countenances.

"Your papers again, Mr. Meyer (that's what they called me), *if* that's your real name."

Once more, I hand over my passport and put my hands on my head.

One of the little thugs leafs through the pages deftly. Uh-oh, he discovers Saudi Arabian visas and others from Egypt and the United Arab Emirates.

"Ah-ha! Your papers are not in order!" he announces loudly and triumphantly. "You will come with us!"

People stare with curiosity and amusement at a tall adult being prodded down a busy street by a miniature militia. I wink at the pedestrians. "*Les petits soldats,*" I mouth to a group of startled French tourists. They smile back.

In order to make the situation more realistic, help the boys think they've captured an honest-to-goodness terrorist; I begin softly chanting the Islamic call to prayer, "*Allah u akbar! Allah u Akbar! Eschedo an la illa ha il allah....*"

We stop at a beautifully-finished, ornate, wooden garden gate after which one of the toe-heads opens, I am ordered to pass through. Inside is a marvelous, high tea style garden party attended by maybe fifty well-dressed people, four of whom upon seeing us dash over with red faces projecting anger and embarrassment.

"Are you all right?" a gentleman asks me with concern. All four cast murderous glances at my captors.

"Fine. Just playing along. Wanted to see what they had in mind for me." I'm hoping, as restitution, I'll be invited to stay, have a few drinks, maybe meet some of these attractive people.

"Okay, then, weareverysorry," the guy says in a rush, and I'm being briskly ushered out by the elbow and expecting a kick in the seat of the pants. The boys are shoe-horned out right behind me.

As the gate slams shut behind us, I hear a frustrated oath, "*Godferdamme!*"

The boys give me these sheepish grins, and I smile back with a Gaelic shrug.

"Why did you start speaking to me in English before you saw my passport?" I asked the mischievous little buggers.

"We can tell you're American."

"How?" Their disclosure floors me because most people I meet overseas assume I'm European. The French almost always speak to me in their language even as I board their air carriers in the US.

"We can just tell." They look at me like I'm dull-witted.

"Well, your English, unlike my Dutch, is excellent. Do you learn it in school?"

"We learn German and French in school. English we learn from television."

We chat for another fifteen minutes, I buy them ice cream, and say *adieu*. I looked back once to wave, but they were busy trying to stop an automobile with their wooden guns.

Familiar friends, who live in Bergen, Wouter and his wife Marianne, drop by my suite with a bottle of single-malt scotch whiskey, which we drink neat. Dinner is also shared at an expensive and delightful bistro after which we go skiing on a man-made mountain with man-made snow substance—some kind of bristly material, rather like thousands of scrub brushes turned upside down. Whatever, the feel and the sound is authentic.

Chapter 3: Around the World in Forty Days

The three of us end the evening playing billiards, the old-fashioned kind with three balls and no pockets, at an upscale downtown bar. Wouter, who knows I have an eye for the attractive Marianne (and so does she), makes it a point to tell me with a wink and a sly grin that, once again, she's going home with him. My admiration for her would have been my secret, but I foolishly told an Austrian associate, and the next thing he does is rat me out with Wouter who, of course, tells Marianne. Now, all three of them gleefully enjoy teasing me at every opportunity. I never get used to their mockery; it's always embarrassing.

Next day, I present a paper in Amsterdam about how to run certain aspects of a multi-national corporation at a week long conference jointly sponsored by International Association of Drilling Contractors (IADC) and Society of Petroleum Engineers (SPE). The venue is a large auditorium with four balconies, which is packed to the rafters. Three large screens hang high above me, the first to my right, the second to my left, each projecting my image. The third in the center projects the visual images from my presentation. The conference members select my paper best-of-the-show, and reward me with an Amstel River dinner cruise where I meet a lovely lady from Spain for some wonderful dinner conversation. Nuff said. That that, Wouter!

Part 3: Germany and Italy

Tom and I drive four hours on the Autobahn at 200 kph (130 mph) to Celle, a charming town in Germany near Hanover, which was fortunately spared the bombs of World War II. The homes, shops, cafes, and cobblestone streets in the business district of old Celle were all constructed between the fourteenth and seventeenth centuries, but they all look as untarnished as if built yesterday. Our purpose is to visit field installations, which we do, but the best part of the day (that would be lunch) is spent eating pig's knuckles and sauerkraut, and drinking beer in our favorite subterranean ratskeller. After completion of our workday, we exercise at a local gym, and run ten kilometers through the streets, which consumes early evening. And the nighttime? Well, let me just say in this day of quick divorces and STDs that one must watch his step. I'll remark a bit later about the enlightened sexual attitude of European women.

Tom returned to Amsterdam and I flew to Genoa where I was met by Gian-Carlo. On the drive to Saline de Volterra, we stopped at Pisa to walk across the Arno and climb the leaning tower. The tower and everything that surrounds it, mainly a baptistery and a mausoleum, including the walkways are made of white marble. It's quite striking.

Saline de Volterra is a walled town that sits on the peak of a hill. Looks like a movie set for *Romeo and Juliet*. The main entry to the village is the original 1000-year-old wooden gate that is now permanently open. Within the walls is an ancient Roman amphitheater estimated to be two thousand years old, which is part of an archeological dig that continues to this day. Early afternoon Gian-Carlo and I are sitting at the main piazza enjoying Comparis and conversing in English. By the way, this area of northern Italy is the hotbed of the Italian Communist Party. Anyway, five burly men who, from their appearance probably work in one of the local alabaster mines, occupy the table to our right. In a high, teasing, singsong voice, one of them calls out in broken English, "Hey, American boy," his voice rising on the last syllable.

The others stifle a laugh. You can kind of see what's going on here. I mean, you know guys… a few drinks after work, and one says, egged on by the others, "Hey, Mauro, I dare you to yada, yada, yada…," and finally he does, with his buddies laughing as much at him as with him.

Chapter 3: Around the World in Forty Days

I smile at Gian-Carlo who does not smile back, him being a sweaty-palm, highly-strung, nervous type threatened by the slightest provocation.

"Hey, American boy." More choked back laughter and snickering.

This time I look directly at them and give them a toothy grin. Gian-Carlo's practically having a seizure.

In unison, they chant, "Gorbachev, Gorbachev, Gorbachev," and collapse with laughter.

I laugh with them, and when Gian-Carlo sees all will be well, he joins in. We spend the remainder of the afternoon drinking and laughing together, our contribution to perestroika.

Part 4: France

I had to fly through Paris to pick up Chuck, coming in from the States, before we continued to Pau, a picturesque hamlet just north of the Pyrenees Mountains that define the Franco-Spanish border. Chuck believes everyone in the world takes pleasure in juvenile-type, southern California humor, so in order to avoid embarrassment (mine) I introduce him to everyone with whom we come into contact, taxi drivers, waitresses, policemen, with a little speech of non-disclaimer: "*Permittez-moi de vous presenter mon ami. Il s'appel, Charles Le-Schlong. Nous habitons aux les Etats Unis, mais il est très bizarre!*" They nod at me knowingly. For the most part it works, but not always.

For example, when boarding a bus for the trip around Paris from Orly to Degaulle to catch the flight to Pau, the bus driver looks at Chuck like he smells horse manure. Chuck responds by calling the guy a fucking frog. Nice. Calm is restored after I wrestle Chuck into his seat. As if to punctuate Chuck's point, the driver gleefully runs a lady off the road, right into the shrubbery, when she tries to merge unto the freeway from an entrance ramp on our right. Chuck gives me an ear-to-ear grin.

"You're right," I sigh. "He's a fucking frog."

The flight to Pau is uneventful until, upon touching down, the overhead bin just ahead of our row opens, and this large, heavy object in a brown wrapper slides out and obeys the law of gravity. About a silly millimeter before it brains this guy ahead of us, Chuck catches it, saving the guy a sure concussion. The guy gives Chuck an irritated sneer, and snatches the package.

Chuck blinks a vacant, confused look, "Nice catch, huh buddy?"

Sneer still in place, the guy comes back with, "No, it was not a nice catch because it was not yours!"

This sets off a number of fucking frog type remarks that threaten to escalate the whole situation into fisticuffs right there on the plane. Fortunately, like most blusterers the guy is a bit of a coward and wants no part of any physical action. The two of them even shake hands, each apologizing (somewhat) for overreacting. I decide to have a little talk with Chuck since we're going to be in Pau the next three days.

"Hey, man, don't take these people personally. They're supposed to be rude. It's their nature."

Chuck looks at me like I'm putting him on. "Really? No way!" he says narrowing his eyes, nostrils flaring. "Are you sure?"

Time for an oil patch style talk.... "Fucking A. They're not treating you any differently than they treat each other. Hell, man, they win trips to the Riviera for being assholes."

Chapter 3: Around the World in Forty Days

Chuck remains skeptical. "I'm not taking any shit from these fucking frogs." He's proud of his alliteration.

"Chuck! Godammit! It's not personal! Just be cool; count to ten; don't react impulsively. Don't be so fucking American."

"Yeah, well.... We'll see...." He's clearly unconvinced.

All goes well until we reach the hotel, and Chuck becomes enamored with the pretty French miss on duty at the front desk. She may be attractive, but has this chill about her, the kind that says to keep your distance. Of course, any kind of subtlety is lost on Chuck. With that in mind, I give her my speech of non-disclaimer mainly to screw Chuck up, but also to distance myself from any of his antics. He tries his charming best to win her over, but she's not buying; in fact, she becomes very icy. Annoyed even. Now Chuck's really confused. He figures the LeSchlong part of my intro refers to him having a talent appreciated by European women, and as promised earlier, here's my take on the fair Continental ladies.

See, you don't have to do the social dance with them—get to know who they are as a person, pretend you're some kind of sensitive metrosexual, wine and dine them until they feel comfortable, share your feelings, bullshit, bullshit, like you do with American women. Just blurt out what's on your mind. Something like, "You like me, I can tell. Would you like to make love?" And by the way, marital status, yours and/or hers, makes no difference.

What is it psychologists say? The same delightful subject recycles through a man's mind about every seven seconds? European ladies seem to know and understand this male quirk; that we have some kind of defective DNA. Anyway, if they agree, you're off to the races. If they disagree, they are not offended, but sweetly tell you no thanks. Ah, but here's hope, guys: American women act a lot differently away from home, which means one must doubly watch his step.

Chuck's nothing if not persistent. The *jolie jeune mademoiselle* has become his weekend project. During dinner he asks me to give him a phrase that will endear him, maybe win her over for some nighttime aerobics. It's no use telling him it's a hopeless cause like fighting China or punching a pillow. His most absurd suggestion is that he tells her she's a monkey woman. Not only would that be too big a mouthful for him to handle, I tell him it sounds stupid. Not even an American female could comprehend what the hell he's talking about. He thinks it's a compliment.

Months later in Bologna, he tries the monkey woman phrase with predictably negative results; although I must admit Franco gave him a slightly different Italian translation. Chuck actually told the lady she looked like a monkey. Franco and I enjoyed the resulting fracas immensely.

Back to Pau. "You could just tell her you like her, *je vous aime*," I suggest.

Chuck tries and tries, but his pronunciation is terrible. It always comes out something like *chavusem*, rather like a sneeze, and the French hate having their language mangled in such a fashion. He even has trouble remembering that short phrase for more than two seconds.

"How about something like, you are very pretty, *vous ettes très jolie?*" I offer. He really murders that.

"Would it be easier to tell her I love her?" he wonders.

"Why the hell would you do that?"

"Hey, it's a trick, you know, a guy trick. So is it easier?"

"Sure, easier, *je t'aime*, but in bad taste. You only use the *tu* form of the pronoun *vous* if the other party is someone you

Chapter 3: Around the World in Forty Days

know very well like a family member or a lover." I consider encouraging him to use the phrase to really piss her off and provide me with entertainment, but empathy (for once) wins out.

"How about if I say I adore her?"

"*Je vous adore*, but that's pushing the envelope." He tries it and once again mangles the pronunciation.

"So, what's the familiar term, the *t'yuuu* term," he giggles, making fun of me.

"*Je t'adore*, but I don't recommend it."

Chuck's eyes light up. He can almost say this one, but it comes out too much like, "shut the door". Finally (and thankfully), he gives up on the whole idea, and we grab a taxi and head to a pub for an after dinner drink or two.

We're standing at the bar, Chuck having a beer and me Pernod with a small pitcher of water. Half way around the bar are four men and two women, fairly young, and starting to feel no pain; not drunk yet, but on the verge. After a while I become aware of some broken English being spoken too loudly, making little sense, but sounding like it's intended to be an insult. We decide to ignore it, figuring it's not intended for us, and continue conversing. The verbal barrage continues even louder, and when I turn to make eye contact, it is apparent that the remarks are intended for Chuck and me.

Sounds vaguely like, "Who tell you come this place, man?"

I decide to investigate, figuring there must be some misunderstanding, mistaken identity—something like that—and walk toward them. Can't imagine anyone not being delighted to see Chuck and me. Three of the guys step toward me, and I think are trying to convey to me in English that our kind aren't welcome in this place. I say something in French about us not being typical ugly American types, and their countenances and attitudes change immediately from hostility to openness and friendship. Turns out, they thought we were British. I later found out that there is tremendous animosity in Pau toward the English, which has existed for several hundred years because a number of rich Brits moved into the big estates and lord it over the locals, or at least used to.

After overcoming the initial confusion, we're playing pool with our new friends, looking at pictures of their children, buying each other drinks, and accepting rides with them to check out other watering holes. Another fellow named Georges joins us who has a pronounced British accent when speaking English, which sounds very odd coming out of a Frenchman. All this time, Chuck is trying to converse with them in something he calls Spanish. Since Pau is near the Spanish border, these folks know the tongue quite well. Georges kindly advises Chuck that that alcohol induced language he is speaking is not Spanish. Chuck retorts that it is a version of Mexican Spanglish, but it sounds like some kind of goofy patois he made up on the spot. Have to admit old Chucko was undaunted and unabashed. No matter how ridiculous he sounded, he just kept on keeping on. What a trooper!

Next morning I'm under the shower nursing a mild hangover and ruing the fact that Thierry is collecting us in thirty minutes. A barrage of shouting and cursing drifts up through the window of my shower from the street below. As I look out to investigate, I become aware that our rooms on the second floor jut out over the main entrance to the lobby. Unable to find the cause of the disturbance, I finish up and head for the lobby to meet Chuck. Pretty soon Chuck comes bounding down the stairs, looks through the open front door where there is a huge puddle and begins laughing.

"Does your shower have an outside window?" he asks. The guy is delighted about something.

Chapter 3: Around the World in Forty Days

"Yeah, sure. Narrow vertical opening from about head level to waist level. Gives a pretty good view."

"Same here. Check it out, I set the shower head for massage and the damn thing sprays like a fire hose; pressure up the wazzoo. While I'm soaping up, I push it to the side and hear all this yelling. I do this maybe three or four times over fifteen minutes. Always yelling and screaming, y'know? I don't connect the two. Finally, as I'm drying off I notice it's been shooting out the window. Now I see this pond by the taxi stand and bus stop. Must've hosed down a few frogs."

Chuck's laughing and talking loudly as he relates this tale, and everyone in the lobby sort of looks at us like we're uncouth foreigners. Well, maybe we are; one of us anyway. Then the lovely desk clerk appears from a back office. I figure this can't be good.

Chucks runs outside, leaps over the puddle, and snatches a handful of flowers from a planter along the boulevard. A sign says anyone disturbing them will go to jail. Chuck runs back to the front desk, hands them to her (dirt falling from the roots all over the floor), and says "Shut the door."

She literally runs for the safety of the back office yelling something like, "*Merde! Cet homme est très stupide, o-la-la!*"

Chuck gives me a vacant, what-the-hell's-wrong-with-her look. "Ah, screw it. She's not worth any more of my time."

The rest of the morning is mostly uneventful, spent talking with the local field engineers about drilling contracts and rig performance in Africa, mainly Gabon and Nigeria. After lunch, a superb duckling served *saignant* (what we would call rare; their rare is *bleu*), we have the rest of the day off, so I call a local tennis club and make a reservation for 1400 (*deux heures*) to play on the red clay. Amazingly and thankfully, for once nothing out of the ordinary happens. We simply play doubles with a couple of young French siblings. In the morning, we'll be off to Cairo.

Part 5: Middle East

Getting through customs in any Middle East country can be a challenge, and Cairo, Egypt is no exception. Fortunately, two fellows from the local office meet our flight and whisk us through the process. Our office is located right on the Nile and we can see the Great Pyramid from our windows. Interesting optical illusion there: the closer you get to the pyramids, the smaller they seem.

The managing director of our Middle East Operation is a mercurial Russian by the name of Rosen Christov, but everyone calls him Rosen Pissed-off. His second in command is an equally volatile Frenchman named Jean-Claude Ouassez (wah-zay). Cairo is headquarters with branch offices in Abu Dhabi, Dubai, and Bahrain. Both are all smiles for Chuck and me, like we're old, lost lodge brothers, but you can kind of feel that neither wants us there, the smiles are not in their eyes, and probably think if they are civil we'll move on faster. Rosen waves us into his office and asks if either of us would like coffee or tea. Chuck opts for the former, and I ask for tea.

Rosen startles us by angrily shouting over the desk and our heads, "Mohammed, you worthless scarab rolling about a ball of camel dung, come!"

This little Egyptian walks in with a pleasant smile and bows slightly, "Yes, Mr. Rosen?"

"Mohammed, coffee, tea! Now! And hurry it up you lazy shit!"

Rosen gives us this benevolent, shit-eating, grinch-like, grin-sneer like we're ignorant in the ways of the world, and in

Chapter 3: Around the World in Forty Days

a very pleasant (but patronizing) voice says, "You have to treat people here that way or they don't respect you."

Mohammed brings in one coffee and two Moroccan teas, my favorite. Just after Chuck and I say thank you, Rosen screams, "Mohammed, you diseased donkey, get out of my office!"

Later, Chuck and I speak with Mohammed who always seems happy and smiling. We suggest he call Rosen Mr. Odious Penis, especially to his face in the presence of others, as it infers great respect in western society; a title of honor. Mohammed is very grateful for the advice. Wish we had been around when that hit the fan.

After the pleasantries with Rosen, we find Mahar, a field engineer, and arrange for him to drive us to Alexandria, but before we can leave, old Pissed-off himself comes running up, clutching a piece of paper in his hands and glaring venom. "Mahar, my friend," he says through clenched teeth. "You are in deep shit." Turns out Rosen found a fax on Mahar's desk, probably placed there by the office secretary. Rosen continues, "You know whenever you receive a fax, I must also have a copy IMMEDIATELY!"

Mahar knots his brow and looks vacantly into space, then with a flourish snatches the fax, bits of the corners still remaining in Rosen's hands. "Aha! I have not seen it! I am off the hook!" With that he throws it over his shoulder, the paper imitating the random path of a falling leaf, and walks to the door, Chuck and me in his wake. As we descend the stairway, the sound of the Russian's violent cursing echoes off the walls. Way to go Mahar!

"Bitchin'," I say.

"Fuckin' A," says Chuck.

Mahar smiles and wags his finger, "No. Foock-ing A, B, C, D, and E.

Several days later, we're packing and preparing to wrap up our visit. Jean-Claude calls our hotel and suggests we have lunch before heading for the airport probably so he can get a download of our impression of the Cairo Operation; see what we're going to tell headquarters.

Our hotel has tennis courts so we take advantage during the morning with two quick sets, get a massage, clean-up, and meet Jean-Claude at a Casbah-type café reminiscent of Rick's Place in *Casablanca*. Alas, no Sidney Greenstreet types are present.

Jean-Claude is railing at the waiter as we arrive. He's unhappy about his table, the menu, the chairs, the rotation of the earth, and on and on. It's embarrassing to have the waiter perceive Chuck and I are of the same ilk, but what can we do? We look at the waiter sympathetically, but it doesn't register. This can only get worse. We're hoping the restaurant staff doesn't piss on our food. Jean-Claude, delighting in our obvious discomfort, reminds us ala Rosen, "They do not respect you unless you treat them like this."

We're not buying his BS. The guy is just an arrogant butthead.

The waiter, a tall reedy guy in a long robe-like garment and a fez, delivers a bottle of wine, and pours a small amount for asswipe to taste. Jean-Claude violently spits the wine on the floor and proceeds to tell the poor guy how terrible it is. Waiter reaches to retrieve the wine and Jean-Claude smacks his hand and tells him to leave it. Turns out, it's actually quite good. The rest of the lunch was also very good, but ruined by the continuing impulsive antics of our host. And they call Americans ugly?

Chapter 3: Around the World in Forty Days

Relative to ugly Americans: Once in Acapulco I was startled by over-the-top offensively rude behavior from an adjoining table. I had never before nor have I since seen such waiter abuse. We had the same waiter. Thinking the diners were American, I felt I should say something.

"I'm really sorry you have to take such abuse. I'm embarrassed for them. Are they New Yorkers?"

"Oh, no sir. They're French. French are much worse than New Yorkers." He paused. "Lousy tippers too."

Back to Cairo. We got to the airport "late;" that is, an hour and a half before our flight, but the boarding area closed thirty minutes before, so now we're stuck in Cairo another day. We check into a hotel by the airport called the Heliopolis, which is crowded with rowdy Israeli tourists, mostly female. I find this surprising, first because it seems a strange place for Jewish women to take a holiday, and second because you'd think they'd maintain a low profile, political and religious passions being what they are in that part of the world.

Chuck and I laze the day away playing tennis and lounging by the pool. In the evening, we take a Nile River dinner cruise hosted by the president of what was then Czechoslovakia. Best dinner cruise I've ever attended, including Hawaii, Amsterdam, New York City — anyplace.

I need to mention that night driving in Cairo is an adventure all to itself. The roadways are jammed day and night; traffic never seems to let up. Sharing the thoroughfares with automobiles are people leading and riding donkeys and camels. Lanes are marked but nobody pays attention. It's common for six to eight cars to squeeze into lanes marked for four. Whatever, it seems to work and traffic moves along efficiently. At night, headlights are not illuminated until someone changes lanes, then they are flashed on and off. Visually, it's a carnival of flashing lights. I asked Mahar, why? He said to save on the battery, then pulled into a petrol station with his lights on, and left them on, while he turned off the engine and dispensed fuel. An enigma for sure, but hey, what, me worry?

Gulf Air booked us to Abu Dhabi via Bahrain, but not until 9:00 p.m., leaving us practically all of the next day to goof off and have dinner before departing for the airport. Tequila had been on our minds since Italy, but in Europe that Agave spirit is a scarce commodity. Mahar dropped by to join us and happened to mention the hotel next door had a café with a Mexican theme. We bopped on over. Well, the restaurant attempted to be Mexican, but it was as if we opened a Mars restaurant based on what we learned talking to a five-year-old. In other words, no tequila, nor anything else that resembled anything Mexican.

The young Egyptian waitress is rather cute so Chuck decides to impress her with his ludicrous Spanglish patois with predictable results. He figures fake Spanish in a fake Mexican café makes sense, which of course only serves to frighten and alienate the waitress. She makes a habit of avoiding our table except for the bare necessities of customer service like dropping off menus and taking the order.

Mahar catches my eye and says lightly with a wink, "I think I prefer Rosen's manners to Chuck's."

"And Jean-Claude's as well?"

"Not Jean-Claude. He is, how you say? A toady? One whose nose is brown?"

"Brownnoser."

"From sticking nose in butt?" Mahar laughs heartily. "That's Jean-Claude. Goes around with nose in Rosen's butt." He laughs until tears roll down his cheeks.

Chapter 3: Around the World in Forty Days

While Mahar and I are enjoying the visual of Jean-Claude and Rosen, Chuck calls the waitress over and says something like *"Donde esta la sala de pisso?"*

He's looking for the restroom, but she doesn't know Spanish and no one knows Chuck's patois. She shakes her head.

Chuck says, "You know....," and then begins making a swishing sound while waving his hand around his crotch area.

I figure we're as good as dead. She bolts away in tears. Mahar is ashen. You see, in Islamic culture one of the greatest insults (maybe the big kahuna) used to degrade women is penis waving, which suggests she is an adulteress and a harlot. I mention this to Chuck to which he says, no way, until Mahar gravely nods. The manager and several other angry males, probably all relatives, throw us out of the establishment.

Now, being associated with oil patch types, getting asked to leave a restaurant is nothing new, but in this part of the world, oil patch trash antics can have harsher consequences. You know, like death?

Mahar, now angry because some of this has rubbed off on him, leaves us to deal with the airport departure procedures on our own, which in Cairo means going through six different passport checks, each official hoping for some kind of bribe. I give one "official" some German marks, me being out of Egyptian and US currency, and he refuses to accept them, I guess figuring it's some kind of "funny" money. Chuck gets a bit fed up at the dance, and resorts to loud fucking A's to communicate his point; whatever it is. As we finally climb aboard a brand new Gulf Air A300 wide-body, I notice we're the only ones in western dress. All other passengers wear *ghutra* and *thobe*, the traditional Arabic dress. I don't see a female among us. One guy walks by with a large bird-of-prey perched on his forearm. I ask if the raptor is a falcon.

"Does eet luke lack a falcon?" he sneers.

"I don't know. I've never seen one."

His countenance changes to one of benevolence for the ignorant infidel who asks stupid questions. "Yes, it is a falcon," he says gently, perhaps remembering the Prophet Mohammed's admonition not to harm people of the book. The "book" is the Holy Qur'an, and the "people" are Moslems, Christians, and Jews, those descended from Abraham.

Bahrain, the first stop, provides more entertainment in the form of a boarding Australian rugby side, about twenty-four of them. These guys look and act like they've been getting jacked-up on beer for several hours. They sing one raunchy song after another, dump pillows on the floor, then put the pillowcases on their heads mocking the Arabs. The Arabs run for seats away from the devils. Finally, a figure of authority, probably their manager, screams for them to sit down and shut up. As we begin the roll for takeoff, one yells in his loudest exaggerated Scottish brogue, "You've got to give me more power, Scotty! I need more power!"

Both Chuck and I are getting huge laughs out of these shenanigans until I see a more sober side. "We're screwed now," I say to Chuck. "When we get to Abu Dhabi, the authorities are going to think we're with these Aussies. Take us three hours to clear customs."

Three hours is a big deal anytime especially when you arrive after midnight, did not arrange to be met by a local to "grease" the procedure, and have to make an eight-hour presentation beginning at 7:00 a.m. This was one time I did not want to be a visionary, but it turns out I was right—to the minute.

It was about 3:00 when I finally got nestled in the sack. Two hours later the *azan*, or call to prayer, erupts so loudly that I damn near fall out of bed. A mosque is located outside my window not three meters away. Just as I was beginning to get oriented, Chuck bangs on my door.

"Hey, let's go for a run!"

"Fuck off!" I yell, but relent and go with him anyway. I feel a bit awkward running the streets in shorts and tank top in the midst of a culture that frowns on such "nakedness." I really rue my decision to join Chuck when he decides to joke around with some armed (AK-47s) guards outside a residence of some local sheikh. You could tell they would have liked to use their weapons on us by their glares of undisguised hatred. Typical Chuck; he thought they liked us.

Later, during our presentation we mention to the guys in the office, six or so who are from Texas, about our quest for tequila. They claim we're in luck because, due to the presence of so many oilmen, Abu Dhabi has an honest-to-goodness authentic Mexican restaurant featuring a dozen or so brands of tequila. Hot damn! We take over the cantina for dinner, opting to stay in the bar and just keep the food and tequila flowing while we swap jokes and war stories with the Texas gang. The evening flies by until they drop us off just in time to catch our flight to Singapore, which departs after midnight (1:30 a.m.).

Part 6: Indo-China

We've got such a good buzz on from the tequila and lack of sleep, that the flaking paint and rust on the fuselage and engine nacelles doesn't faze us. The long climb up the outside steps into a wheezing old 747 is a challenge in our semi-inebriated condition. Neither of has heard of the carrier, Garuda, which we decide is Malay for Garbage Air. Later we find out it's some kind of bird. Maybe it's a garbage eater. The aircraft is only about half full, so we plan on grabbing some extra seats and sacking out for most of the twelve-hour flight. Unfortunately, the cabin we're in also contains about forty chain-smoking Frenchmen. To make matters worse, when we reach cruising altitude the air-handling system is turned off to conserve fuel. To make matters really worse...

"Hey, Swartz," says Chuck—we had just started calling each other Swartz (me) and Schwartz (him) as in, May the Schwartz be with you (from *Space Balls*), "Did you check out of the hotel?"

"Oh, shit...."

Somewhere in an Abu Dhabi hotel alongside a mosque are two rooms, each containing a suitcase full of clothing, toiletries, tennis racquets, and other things interesting. Fortunately, we kept our briefcases with us since we went directly from the office to the cantina to the airport.

Air filled with putrid cigarette smoke sticks to my clammy body for the entire flight and combines with lack of sleep to turn me into a zombie-like state, which is miserable but paradoxically seems to hasten the twelve hour flight. The Frenchmen run for the door as soon as the 747's tires touch runway, and queue up before the plane reaches the jet-way. Flight attendants couldn't care less.

First thing we do upon deplaning is call the office in Abu Dhabi, have them check us out of the hotel, and ship our luggage to the Houston headquarters office. In Singapore it's a glorious day, and Changi Airport may be one of the most beautiful in the world. Neither of us is in the mood to go shopping, so upon checking into the concierge level of the Crown Plaza Hotel on Orchard Boulevard, we don robes over our bikini briefs (which resemble Speedos if you don't look too carefully), and veg out at the Olympic-size swimming pool on the roof. The pool is surrounded by tropical flora of all colors and types, including palm trees, and has an attractive open air bar, café, and pool shop. The deck chaise lounges are padded and covered with thick terrycloth, and I have no trouble fall-

Chapter 3: Around the World in Forty Days

ing asleep. Sometime later, the touch of cool, refreshing water awakens me.

"Hey, Swartz, come on in. You're getting a sunburn." Chuck and three attractive women from Australia are splashing me from the pool.

Good idea. I feel well rested, but definitely a bit overheated, Singapore being located almost smack dab on the equator. Just before I dive in, Chuck points out to the Aussies that I'm sporting underwear, which they find very amusing. I remind Chuck he is too. "So are you, Schwartz."

"Nuh-uh!" he says, and hops on the side of the pool displaying a snazzy blue-and-green striped Speedo purchased from the pool shop while I lay asleep.

"Does eet luke lack a falcon?" he sneers, trying to imitate the raptor-toting Arab on the Abu Dhabi flight, but ruins the effect with inane giggling, although it makes the effect more irritating, which was probably his goal anyway.

Later, after emerging from the cool, refreshing water, I wrap my robe around me and furtively slink to the pool shop for a similar purchase. Later in the day, Schwartz and Swartz (same pronunciation since Germans pronounce "s" like "sch," but Chuck and I argue about the spelling) go shopping for enough clothing to get through the rest of the trip. Singapore is wide open on Sunday, just another day for commerce. Although they do not claim Islamic status, like neighboring Malaysia, it is the prevailing religion. Islam requires one to rest for a half-day on Friday, and Saturday is the Sabbath. On returning to the hotel we meet three women from Washington DC on vacation, and have them join us for a beer in a nearby bar where we meet another businessman from Germany. The six of us palled around for the next two days, which made the stay even more pleasant.

By the end of our time, we ditched Gunter, the German, who became a real bore, always blathering on about intricate business and stock market transactions. The guy was a one-trick pony whose aim was to impress, not communicate, at least not in a way that facilitated freely flowing discourse among peers. The DC ladies flew to Bali, Chuck went to Thailand and Vietnam, and I headed for Kuala Lumpur (KL), Borneo, and Perth, Australia. The plan was for Chuck and me to meet back in Singapore in one week and return to the US together.

KL was only twenty minutes by air, and was the meeting place for myself and several from the home office. Our ultimate destination was Sarawak where I was to present a technical paper to the local SPE Chapter. I met the others at the KL Hilton where we stayed overnight, and flew to Borneo early the next morning.

Upon landing, we drive through the State of Brunei, right past the Sultan of Brunei's golden mosque, and into Sarawak. My presentation is uninspired, flat, and dull, something that frequently happens when I am completely at ease and relaxed. I need a bit of an edge, some nervous energy to give an entertaining performance, as I had in Amsterdam. Dull or not, I receive a rousing ovation from a surprising large crowd, maybe three hundred, and they present me with a beautiful carving of a Borneo headhunter, which occupies a spot of honor on my desk to this very day. I feel a bit guilty accepting it, giving such a half-assed performance.

Part 7: Australia

Perth is one of my favorite places, having the climate San Diego claims as its own. I check into the Burswood Island Casino and am a bit startled and delighted to be met by John Speed, the Operations Manager for Australia who lives and is headquartered in Sydney. Sydney to Perth is like New York to Los Angeles. Thirty seconds later I'm surprised when Chuck

Chapter 3: Around the World in Forty Days

comes sauntering up, zipping up his fly and catching my accusing eye.

"I washed my hands. Just forgot to zip. Don't want the trouser monster to get out."

"What the hell are you doing here, Schwartz?" I wonder, but I'm delighted to see him.

"Finished up early, Swartz. Thought I'd give you a hand with the presentation in Fremantle."

"Outstanding. I hate doing all day myself."

"Pretty boring for those listening too."

"Fuck you. I hope you caught the clap in Vietnam."

"Maybe," Chuck winks at Speed.

I look at John. "You were there too?"

John says, "Did you know mattresses look just like falling leaves when launched from ten floors up?"

"I don't want to know," I sighed, thankful that I was not with them.

Speed rang up another associate and arranged for us to play tennis doubles. Chuck and I had to borrow racquets from the pro shop since ours were on the way home. We played on both grass and synthetic grass. The latter surface was strange in that the ball stayed low, like on grass, but rebounded slowly, like on clay. Later that evening, Chuck and I meet two Aussie sisters in the casino. They filled us in on several local gambling games, and suggested sights for us to check out while in the Perth area. Thankfully Chuck was on good behavior or was he just tired?

I opt for a fifteen kilometer run at 6:00 the next morning, eat a light breakfast, and catch a taxi for the office in Fremantle. Chuck and John departed earlier; neither in the mood to run after all the spirits consumed the day and night before, which is precisely why I did run. The cabby is an Italian ex-pat who is excited about the annual tennis tournament at Burswood, featuring the top male and female players in the world in a format of mixed double arranged by nationality. He mistakes me for someone having to do with the tournament. Guy then tells me he used to me an opera singer in Italy, which he pronounces, It-lee with emphasis on the first syllable. I react with skepticism. He proceeds to show me. He's an old guy, probably mid-seventies, with a voice that's fifty years younger. First, he lays on me some requiem mass liturgy number, says he still performs for the church, then an aria from *Faust*. Knocked me out. I could have listened to him all day. The greatest singer in the world, whoever he was—and I never caught his name.

Part 8: Going Home

Our original "revised" plans were to return to the US through Sydney, but all the Aussie domestic airlines went on strike without warning, so we returned to Singapore for an overnight, and a flight to Los Angeles through Tokyo. In the queue at Changi the following morning, we meet two very pleasant Brazilian ladies who are sharing our flights all the way to LAX, and depart for Rio de Janeiro from there. This turns out to be rather fortunate for them because their native tongue was lost on the gate agent who was fluent in all the nearby Asian languages and English, but Portuguese? Not so much. Chuck and I helped them get the flight arrangements squared away. For once we were actually good Samaritans.

The flights become memorable in that Chuck and I tried to find out as much as possible about hot vacation spots in Brazil, and they were equally curious about the U.S. Verbal communication was very poor, but all four of us kept on trying. I suppose there was little else to do, what with neither Swartz nor Schwartz knowing Portuguese, and neither of the Brazil-

Chapter 3: Around the World in Forty Days

ians speaking much English. I pleaded (begged!) with Chuck to lay off the patois to avoid alienating them. *Vive le différence, n'est-ce pas?* An appropriate ending to a great trip.

Epilogue

While Los Angeles International Airport was a welcome sight (always great to get home), it was disconcerting to see what has been happening to our citizens. I mean, the malady was there all along, but I guess it took getting out of the country and returning so I could see with new eyes. Anyway, it was obvious that we have become the land of the oddly shaped and poorly dressed. Not one pair of pants fit properly or had a crease. Shirts, mostly tees, fit like tents. I wonder if American kids would think shorts that come below their knees are "so cool" if they knew the Arabs have been wearing them as swimming suits for decades, anything shorter considered indecent.

What a nation of slobs we've become. Sloppy teen-aged girls oozed around wearing hip-hugging jeans displaying ample, quivering, guts blobbing out of their naked midriffs. There were more morbidly obese people at LAX than I saw the entire trip around the planet; adults and children alike, male and female, all stuffing their faces in a continuing ritual of self-destruction.

"Y'all go on over and gitcher self a pizza slice," one youngish, humongous father said handing his roly-poly ten-year old some money.

"I want some fries," protested the kid.

"Listen, I don't want you spending money on junk food. 'Sides, you git extra bread sticks with the pizza."

One red-faced XXXL Wagnerian-type lady was sitting on a bench looking distressed. I asked if I could assist, get her some help, maybe some water.

She looked up and said, "Lordy, lordy, lordy. I just don't know why my feet hurt."

What a hanging curve ball, just begging to be hit out of the park. What a straight line. It took all the self-control I could muster, but gentleman that I am, I bit my tongue.

I understand tort lawyers in our country have now decided fast food may be the next "tobacco opportunity"; that McDonald's and others have conspired to force people to consume mass quantities of fat laden food. The bastards!

But wait a minute! Before I condemn what has happened in our society, I see an opportunity to pile on. That's right, my quirks and overall smart-alecky condition are the results of society not providing enough education or seminars or some other psych-babble liberal bullshit. You fill in the blank. My God, I even had to play dodge-ball in grade school. No wonder I'm the way I am. I decide from then on, I have no responsibility for any of my own actions. That's right; I'm a victim! What a revelation! In the immortal last word of William Wallace, FREEDOM!

I feel a tug at my sleeve that jerks me out of my reverie. The fat lady looks up at me and says with a meaningful sigh, "I just don't know why I'm so short of breath."

Now just being set free, I couldn't let that one pass. "That's because," I said, "most things your size have an engine."

Hey, don't blame me. It's not my fault I have no self-control, manners, or empathy. I'm a victim of my environment, remember?

But don't worry, citizens. This too shall pass.

Chapter 4

Weekend Excursion

I FINISHED my business in Pau, a picturesque French hamlet located just north of the Pyrenees Mountains. This natural border separates France from the Iberian Peninsula. It was late Thursday afternoon, job completed a full day earlier than expected. My flight to Bologna was booked for a Saturday departure and arrival, but then what? Sit around until Monday morning? Sounded like the old American axiom of hurry up and wait. There had to be another course of action; something that would enhance quality of life—mine of course.

Within the hour, a helpful hotel concierge replaced my air tickets with rail passage, as follows: leave Pau Friday morning and travel along the French Riviera through Nice and Cannes, spending overnight and all day Saturday in Marseilles. Departure from Marseilles was scheduled for Sunday morning with a change of trains at the Italian border. From there the journey would continue to Milan in part along the Italian Riviera. I was required change trains again in Milan, gambling on a rather tight timetable, and scheduled to arrive in Bologna in time for

Chapter 4: Weekend Excursion

Sunday dinner. I wired the Italian office about my change of plans, and congratulated myself for the foresight.

Two associates, Graham from Aberdeen, Scotland, and Dub from Houston, Texas also decided to cancel their flights and horn in on my excursion. At first I was sorry I mentioned it to them, being rather annoyed with the prospect of having my planned solitude disturbed. But one mustn't be selfish about sharing a quality-of-life experience, must one? That's me: a real humanitarian.

The following day, a beautiful Friday summer morning was gorgeous and arid; perfect for a rail trip along the Mediterranean. The train wasn't in the class of the ultra-modern, 200 mph TGV I frequently took from Paris, but it was comfortable with classy furnishings and excellent service. Most of the journey featured an unblocked view of the sea, an unexpected and welcomed benefit. We stopped at both Nice and Cannes to disembark and take on passengers. I regretted that I had to remain on board, and made a mental note to make this journey again, allowing several days stay at both villages. I could practically hear the Siren's call: the lure of laughter, the sound of sun-splashed surf, the smell of the sea.

By late afternoon, probably about four-thirty, we pulled into the station at Marseilles, the day still glorious; more so with longer shadows that produced added contrast and made colors seem more vivid. Ah, Marseilles, birthplace of bouillabaisse; and I was anxious to get some.

After checking into l'Hôtel Sofitel a short time later, Graham, Dub, and I met at the swimming pool bar to eyeball *les jolies filles* getting their boobs a suitable shade of tan. *Je veux seulement oublier, vous savez?* See, the thing is to sneak furtive glances, you know, like it's no big deal. Graham and I were both master voyeurs. Not Dub. First trip abroad, y'see? Anyway, old Dub's eyes are practically popping out of their sockets, and I could tell by his squirming that he had major wood in his pants. Not only that, but the woody formed pointing the wrong way; down-leg rather than up-leg. Guys, you know what I'm talking about.

One of the young ladies decided to leave the pool for the day, and passed by the bar with perky knockers on high beams. She noticed Dub's salivating stare, and with sort of a half-smile, shook her head. She turned to me, the guy with the nonchalant, couldn't-care-less *visage*, pointed to Dub and said,

"*Americain, n'est-ce pas?*"

"*Mais bien sur*," I said with a Gaelic shrug. I was pretty sure Dub had a visual that would keep him "up" that night.

And dinner? The bouillabaisse? Brack! P'tui! Terrible! Worst I'd ever had! Loaded with bony fish parts and spiny urchin-like creatures, greasy broth—absolute swill! On the other hand, the bread and wine were superb, and the marina in the heart of the port was alive with activity, as were the pubs. Most of the latter were caught up in a televised soccer tie between their hometown team and Toulouse. I managed to have an enjoyable evening notwithstanding the rancid fish soup.

The next day, Saturday, was free so after a light breakfast of croissants, marmalade, and orange juice, we swam in the pool, checked out the boobs, er, girls, basked in the sun, and talked a little business. Just before midday, Dub said he'd like to pick up souvenirs for his family. After a quick change we strolled downtown to a picturesque sidewalk café where we ate a leisurely lunch featuring several bottles of wine. Dub snapped photographs non-stop throughout the day, except at the swimming pool.

Sometime during our metropolitan shopping crawl, we unintentionally walked down a side street that interspersed souvenir shop and girlie clubs. One of these, the Las Vegas Club, had three tall, gorgeous, scantily clad, well-endowed, black girls fronting the joint. The called out to male passers-by

Chapter 4: Weekend Excursion

in husky, come hither voices, the idea being to get lonely, perverted, or horny souls to come-on-in and separate them from as much money as possible. From their accents, I guessed they were from Cameroon. Whatever, they were knock-outs. They were probably good at what they did, just like piranha.

About that time I got an idea. Looking back, I realize it was not a good one, but what the hell, live and learn. I kind of signaled one of the girls, motioning my head toward Dub, while telling her she is very beautiful (*très belle*). Before I get the words completely out, she attempted to press up against me, started talking breathlessly, and tried to pull me toward the club. Talk about an unintended result! As efficiently as possible (and somewhat breathlessly) I extracted myself (with a too loud "Not me!"), and explained that Dub is a sex-deprived, wealthy American who had always wanted an African girl, but was afraid to ask. In a flash, all three are on him, fondling his hair, and rubbing his chest. They also tried to drag him into the club. I noticed he dropped his camera.

Poor Dub was frightened shitless, but you could tell he was strangely enjoying the experience, though not wanting to. While Graham pretended to be trying to rescue him, I began snapping pictures with Dub's camera as fast as I could. Dub was oblivious to my handiwork, but the girls weren't. They really played it up, leaving several vivid lipstick marks on Dub's face. Some of my shots had to be real "keepers." Just before Graham extricated him, I snuck the camera back into the fallen case. Dub was actually shaking a bit and sweating when I returned the case to him.

"Hope it wasn't damaged in the fall." I was all concern and empathy.

He checked it out carefully, still trembling slightly. "Looks okay." Then, "Damn, what did you tell them?"

"Just that we weren't interested... that you're a family man... that we're looking for souvenirs for your wife and kids in America... that sort of stuff," I lied. "Probably thought of you as a unique challenge."

Graham, who understands French, tried to keep a straight face (and mostly succeeded) during my prevarication and allowed that he almost lost the battle what with three on one. The way he winked at me I was pretty sure he got a schwantz massage as well. Dub wondered what the hell I was doing during all the commotion. I explained sheepishly that I was frightened—after all they attacked me first—and made a run for it before I realized what happened. I acted all sorry like for being a coward, but mentioned that I did return in time to prevent them from stealing his camera. Dub offered me a sincere thank you. I said no problem. Graham was practically peeing his pants.

At the time (and here's why it was a bad idea), I figured Dub would give the film to his wife to have it developed. If so, it would be also safe to assume she would pick up the prints and be the first to view them. I could visualize the outcome: Let's see... the Pyrenees, a charming hotel, some historic monuments, a sidewalk café, a picturesque marina, and WHA??? I could just hear Dub doing Jackie Gleason's Ralph Kramden character, "Hamana, hamana, hamana," and wondering who took the shots. If asked, I would tell him some guy handed the camera to me after it fell when I returned from my attempted, if shameful, escape.

The following morning, we were on our way again enjoying the view of sails and bathers on the Riviera. About midday, we entered Italy, left the French conveyance, and boarded a rickety, smelly, Italian train loaded to the gills. The process was confusing, and it took about half an hour to accomplish the transfer. I forgot that we would be crossing the border the last day of August, the very day everyone in Italy would be re-

Chapter 4: Weekend Excursion

turning from holiday. Not only was there standing room only, the train was painfully slow, maybe thirty-five mph. However, part of the trip was along the Italian Riviera so we enjoyed an outstanding view. Some buck-naked guys got a kick out of standing tall and waving hands and penises at the train. Oddly, the Italian beaches consisted mostly of driveway-type stones, not sand.

We arrived in Milan just in time to make a desperate run for our connection, only to watch the train pull away. No worries, though, since another train to Bologna was scheduled to depart several hours later. The station was very chaotic, what with the heavy returning holiday traffic. Being Sunday, the currency exchange kiosks were closed; something else I/we failed to anticipate. In addition, the currency machines we found were out of order. Again, no worries since we could exchange money after we arrived at our hotel in Bologna or at a bank Monday morning. I was wrong about the "no worries" part. Lack of lire turned out to be a significant "worry."

About a half hour south of Milan, the conductor requested our tickets. Naturally, we handed over those for the train we missed. By the look on his face we could clearly tell something was amiss. I pegged the conductor as being a cheerful chap under normal circumstances; however the stress of the returning hoard had obviously taken its toll. At any rate, he was clearly agitated with us as he attempted to point out some kind of error. Neither of us spoke Italian, and he knew no English. The lack of a common verbal communication medium annoyed him even further. After failed attempts at sign language combined with some goofy made-up patois, Graham said something to me, unaware it was in French, out of exasperation. Something like we were in a tough spot. The conductor replied, *"Ah, nous connaisson Francais! Maintenant, nous pouvent parler."*

Our relief was short-lived. He explained that we owed additional fare; roughly the equivalent of forty US dollars each because this particular train had Pullman cars. It didn't matter whether or not one was assigned a berth; the fare structure was determined by the train configuration. We had no lire, and he would not accept American greenbacks—a complete surprise and object lesson to us. Finally, the conductor completely lost patience, had spent enough time with us, and said he would stop the train immediately and put us off. He reached for the cord to signal the engineer, when Graham, remembering the communication lesson, asked if Francs were acceptable. Turned out they were. Fortunately, Graham had enough to cover us.

We arrived at Bologna just after dark. The hotel was a short taxi ride away. In the lobby waiting for us (an unexpected and welcome surprise) was Franco Arbizanni, the controller of our entire Italian operation: sales in Bologna and manufacturing in Saline de Volterra. A real gentleman, Franco didn't want us to dine alone, and besides he loved food and entertaining. If he was being a bit self-serving, it served us even better. Anyway, we got into his Volvo, and to put us in the proper frame of mind, Franco slipped in a CD that featured arias by Pavarotti. He cranked up the volume.

The meal was festive, fraternal, and loud, mainly thanks to our expansive host who strikes an amazing resemblance to Benito Mussolini—an opinion left unsaid for obvious reasons. We started with a crisp, chilled, white wine before dinner, then a hearty red with a nine-course meal. Each course was small, maybe just right is a better description, so at the end one felt sated but not stuffed. For a digestif, Franco preferred Fernet Branca, a putrid inky liquid, but the rest of us opted for grappa, which tastes a bit like kerosene, but has a soothing aftereffect.

We ended the evening by the four of us taking a leak from a low wall at the rear of the café, down into a yawning ravine. We had a competition to see who could squirt the longest and the farthest. I won the longest competition.

Chapter 4: Weekend Excursion

The next morning was sun-splashed, crisp, and refreshing with just the slightest hint of a perfumed breeze. It was the kind of morning all mornings should be. A "thank God I'm alive" kind of morning. That kind of realization often leads me in an opposite direction, which is contrary to my normally bright mood. That is, I think ruefully of similar mornings that will occur after I pass beyond the veil of this life. Makes me a bit sad to acknowledge I'll be missing out on an event that some future human form may not appreciate. With that in mind, I decided on a leisurely stroll to the office rather than a taxi, the idea being to extend my "alone time" in that wonderful atmosphere, a morning that would never come again, on a day that was one day closer to my end; damn, there I go again!

I stopped for about half an hour at an outdoor café for pastry and orange juice, and simply watched people go bustling by. I was absolutely at peace. After another relaxing stroll of about twenty minutes, I entered our office and proceeded to a gaily-decorated conference room. Cake, iced champagne, and the office staff awaited our guest of honor, Ernie Gugger, our Italian Operations Managing Director. He's a small, gray-haired, bright, articulate individual originally from Switzerland. Ernie is fluent in nine languages, and a skilled but charming negotiator. For this reason, our company required him to make numerous trips around the Eastern Hemisphere to maintain and expand our business relationships and strategic alliances.

That particular day Ernie was being honored by his staff for returning safely from Iraq about a month and a half previously. They would have feted him sooner, but decided to wait for my arrival. You see, the two of us had embarked to Baghdad for a two-day trip, but simultaneous to our arrival, Saddam Hussein decided to round up foreign nationals and hold them as his "guests." As fate would have it, we got caught in the web. Some of our fellow prisoner/guests were beaten and punched during our ordeal, but fortunately we were held prisoner part of the time in our own offices. Fortunate because although the Iraqis cut off telephone access, they forgot about fax machines. Ernie sent day-to-day, breathtaking accounts of our incarceration and the events that ensued. Finally, after eight days, Saddam's henchmen loaded us on buses and headed west for four brutally hot, angst-filled hours. We were dumped off in the middle of the desert and abandoned. After several hours enduring incredible heat, members of the Syrian Army picked us up, and allowed us to proceed home. Talk about a road trip!

And so, we tipped several glasses to Ernie and gave thanks for our safe return. Graham returned to bonny Scotia, Dub to Texas, and I headed for Singapore.

Chapter 5

Saddam's Guest

I WOKE in a stupor of foggy disorientation. At best I had received maybe three hours of restless sleep. Most of the night, I lay awake, tossing and turning, and attempted to ignore the oppressively sticky heat and the sour smelling cot. Then there was the reality that I might never see home and family again.

I knew it was almost sunrise because I heard the *azan*, the call from the muezzin for first prayer, resonate from the minarets throughout the region. The first line declared that God was greater than.... That's the context: dot, dot, dot. The inference is God is greater than anything one could possibly name or conjure up. The *azan* also encouraged the faithful to hurry to prayer; and rush to success.

The sleeping quarters, for seventy of us, was a large cavernous building that was an old airplane hangar with the big doors partially open at one end. Open or not, there was no air movement within the structure. There was also no insulation under the tin roof. The place was an oven. Our cots, bare save for worn, dirty sheets covering urine-stained, thin mattresses,

Chapter 5: Saddam's Guest

were arranged in a square pattern, seven by ten, with perhaps two and a half feet between cots.

I sat up groggily. My God, it tasted like the entire Republican Guard had marched through my mouth barefoot. An involuntary yawn was a bit too loud, which caught the attention of Tariq, who quickly stood and readied his AK-47.

Tariq, like all of our guards, tried to look like a Saddam clone: same military clothing, same black beret, and same moustache. He had probably been half snoozing in his chair when I caused the disturbance. His beret had been removed, and why not? Who could wear a hat in this heat? I couldn't help but notice, sans beret, he had scant resemblance to tennis great, Andre Agassi. When he took notice of my confused state, his face softened a bit, and we made eye contact.

"*Sabach al-hair* (good morning)," I said quietly.

"*Sabach noor* (bright morning)." Surprised at my greeting, he replied (almost) pleasantly.

I gestured at him and smiled thinly. "Andre Agassi." This was pushing the envelope a bit. It could piss him off.

"Me? Agassi?" He grinned broadly.

"*Nam* (yes). Agassi's father was a wrestler on the Iranian Olympic team back in the seventies," I offered.

"Then he was Shiite like me," Tariq beamed. "Agassi is Shiite?" He asked.

I knew he wasn't, but said, "Oh, Yes!"

Tariq continued to grin, and I thought I might have made somewhat of a friend, if there could be such a thing under the circumstances. Tariq must have later repeated our conversation to his peers because from that time on the other guards referred to him as Agassi, which always seemed to delight him.

"You come," he beckoned. "Bring ablutions things."

I picked up my toiletries kit and followed him to the only bathroom in the building. He stood outside the doorway as I removed my underwear and splashed water from head-to-toe, applied deodorant, slipped back into my dirty skivvies, and brushed my teeth. It was the nicest thing he could think of to do for me, and I appreciated it. He escorted me back to my cot.

"*Shukran* (thank you)," I said sincerely.

"*Afwan* (you're welcome)," he smiled.

Last week seemed like an eternity ago. Ernie Gugger and I had flown into Baghdad from Bologna to confer with the Iraqi oil minister. We decided to stop at our local office before checking into our hotel, and were there accosted by the Iraqi Militia who herded us and all other building occupants into waiting buses. Arms and legs were shackled. Like us, the other building occupants represented either European-based or American-based firms, mostly having to do with oil drilling or servicing. Though most of us were westerners, the militia brought along our local staff as well; anyone present at the time.

We had a small fifth-floor office normally staffed by an engineer, Alfred Kanon, an Iraqi Christian, an office clerk, Latif Zilka, an Iraqi Jew, and an Iraqi government liaison specialist, Mehdi Katani, a Shiite originally from Iran. Again, they were not allowed to return to their families in Baghdad, but were sequestered with us. Of all of us, the local workers seemed most distraught, and we spent a lot of time comforting them—or trying to anyway. Some of Latif's relatives had been executed over the years, so the Iraqis' distress was from anticipation of history being repeated while ours was mostly from fear of the unknown.

However, our bus did include one soft, fleshy, sniveling bureaucrat who said he worked for a US senator from Ver-

Chapter 5: Saddam's Guest

mont. Said his name was Robert Vecsey like it should mean something. He loudly denounced US attitudes about Islam and Iraq. Said he and his boss were advocates of Saddam. He went on to complain that he did not belong with our ilk, and demanded special treatment. He got it in the form of a punch in the mouth from one of the guards. Guy actually started crying. I could understand that he was frightened. Hell, we all were. But I also pegged him as one who would throw all of us under the bus to save his own skin.

Our passports and all other possessions were confiscated. We were only allowed to keep the clothes on our backs, and our toiletry articles. After a bumpy and dusty ride of maybe forty-five minutes, we were delivered to the hangar, and told to align by nationality. We did some meaningless circling but remained with our office mates. The guards could have arranged us using our passports, but seemed bored, so as long as we acted like we were obeying they were satisfied.

The guard, whom I later learned was Tariq, confronted Ernie and shouted, "What is your country?"

"Switzerland." That was true.

"And you?" he said to me.

"Switzerland." Well, my family immigrated to America from Switzerland.

He moved on....

Now it was the next morning after my sink bath courtesy of Tariq. The guards prodded everyone awake and motioned to a long table at the opposite end of the hangar from the big doors. On it were fifteen-inch rounds of pita bread, still warm, some baklava, Arabic coffee, and juice. After eating, mostly in silence, at the insistence of the guards ("No talking!"), we were shackled and roughly man-handled into two waiting buses. Those who stumbled were rewarded with a punch or a kick.

Vecsey was scared shitless, and we all took some pleasure in his discomfort, smiling slightly and winking at each other; our form of gallows humor. The guy never stopped trying to set himself apart from the rest of us (as being ashamed of America and on the side of Saddam); a typical self-serving bureaucrat who valued politics without principles. His efforts only distanced him further from us and our captors; but being totally clueless, he continued sounding off like an anti-American ugly American. How's that for a paradox?

The heat took no holiday in the early morning as we bumped along, stopping at various check points, until an hour later, the buses stopped in front of our office building, a modern seven-story, square granite structure with ample windows.

On the first day, the guards loudly ordered us into the street, punching those who were slow, and taking rifle butts to those who fell. We were taken into the building, and told to remain in our offices for the rest of the day until they came once again to collect us. Naturally, they left armed guards at all points of egress.

We all welcomed the thought of veging out and trying to make sense of what was happening in air-conditioned comfort, but the air handling system had been shutdown, and the telephones removed as well. We still hadn't been told why we were being held. Any question was met with a fist or a boot. I figured if I could get Tariq to warm up a bit he might tell me something in a private moment, but any kind of private moment did not seem probable. Still....

Ernie returned from the toilet with darting eyes and swiveling head. He looked at me and spoke quietly and furtively.

"They forgot about the fax machine."

"You're kidding!" A ray of hope.

"No, it's still here, and operating too."

Chapter 5: Saddam's Guest

"Who should we contact? Head office?"

"I think we should fax Bologna," said Ernie, "because they're only a time zone away. They can get the word out to everyone else."

Made sense, so we did, Ernie using Italian because he said our captors only understood Arabic, French, and English. I figured Ernie should know, being a veteran of the practically everywhere in the world and fluent in nine languages.

"Hell, Ernie, I don't think it matters. If we're caught they won't give a rat. Probably hang you up by your thumbs until you tell them what it says."

"I'm a good story-teller," he said cheerfully; more cheerful than the situation warranted.

For the rest of that day and those following, we faxed back and forth, not using the handset in case someone was listening. We shredded all outgoing messages and incoming replies. It felt better that people knew what had happened to us if not why.

In late afternoon the guards came back, put us in irons, and loaded us back on the buses. After a week of this routine, one particular day was different in that the drivers aimed into the afternoon sun, the opposite direction from our hangar. Any attempt at conversation with each other or a guard was met swiftly with brutality. The heat was incredible; we were all perspiring freely, some close to being dangerously ill. Two-hours later, many of us including Vecsey, needed a bathroom break. We hoped the guards did as well.

"Gentlemen, please, I need to go to the bathroom," pleaded Vecsey. For once, we sympathized, and gave him a mental "attaboy" for speaking up, especially when none of us had the courage.

"Shut up or die!" yelled the nearest guard whom I later learned was Rashid. Later in the day, one of our number addressed him as Rajab, which earned a severe beating. A Moslem male resents having his name mispronounced, looks at it as gross disrespect. He made his victim say his name over and over until he passed out. Mr. Rashid, Mr. Rashid, Mr. Rashid.

"But I really have to go. I can't hold it anymore."

"You piss in pants, you piss on bus, you die!"

Another several hours later, the buses stopped and we were pushed into the hot desert and told to relieve ourselves. Though the guards had water, we were given none. The guards kept looking to the west as if expecting something. After another hour of waiting (for what?) under the blazing sun, they put us back on the buses and returned to the hangar four hours the opposite direction. By now, even the guards and drivers were totally spent. At the hangar we were given water and pita bread then collapsed on our cots. Heat and all, I slept fitfully.

The muezzin's call woke me the following morning. Again, as I sat up, I noticed Tariq.

"Agassi," I nodded and gave a little salute.

"Yes. Come do ablutions."

Once again I followed him to the bathroom thankful for his kindness. As we returned, he stepped back in stride with me, and whispered, "You sponsor me to America?"

"You know I'm not Swiss?"

"I look at passport."

"Sure, I'll be your sponsor." What else could I say?

"You have card for number I contact?"

"At the office."

Chapter 5: Saddam's Guest

"*Alhamdalela* (Thank God for everything). Good. We go again today." He swiftly stepped off before I could ask him why we were being held.

Well, I never heard from Tariq after that day, though he did receive my business card. I suspected he was killed in one of the Gulf Wars. *Insha-allah* (God's will).

Once again at the office, Ernie and I were busy with the fax machine. Turned out none of our government officials, American, Italian or Swiss intended to do a damn thing. Our Bologna office said the only advice they offered was to endure, hang in there, bullshit, bullshit.... International tensions being what they were, etc., etc., bullshit, bullshit....

"Well, that's hopeful," I said with sarcasm.

"At least they know we're here and being held captive. Things change you know. Stay positive, my friend."

I discovered a real strength in Ernie. Never during our captivity did he outwardly seem discouraged. He was the first to offer comfort and an encouraging word to any of us who needed bucking up. The guards even showed some deference to him.

We spent the morning writing Bologna letters to pass onto our families and co-workers, but only in case of the worst. Tried to make out like we were some kind of heroes, but truth to tell, we were no better than that weasel Vecsey. Not really.

The guards, Tariq absent, returned at noon with a liter of water for each of us, loaded us on the buses, and once again set out to the west. We anticipated another steam bath-like, four-hour trip and were not disappointed. When we were unloaded in the desert, I think most of us expected to be shot and left. When we looked into each other's vacant faces it was like we knew we were looking at dead men.

Our manacles were removed, and we were forced to sit in a circle (facing out) on our hands. The desert floor blistered my fingers. The guards were at our backs.

What was there to say? What was there to do? It was helpless and the situation was hopeless. All I could think of was to make peace with God, but try as I might I could not focus on a prayer. I felt an overwhelming sadness.

After some indeterminate time, without a word, our guards boarded the buses hastily and left in a cloud of dust. Some time later the Syrian Army arrived and escorted us over the border. We were safe. We were going home.

Epilogue

We discovered later that it was Saddam himself who arranged our release, not any of our western governments. Apparently, once he decided to take us prisoner, he didn't know what else to do so he set us free. Guy must've been bi-polar. Go figure.

Chapter 6

The Operation

THE FLIGHT from Paris, my final stop on this trip, to Houston has been pleasant with good conversation, wine, and food. The only thing missing is candlelight. My next to last stop was Amsterdam where I was strip searched at the airport because my passport contained a number of stamps and visas from the Middle East. I did not mind their suspicion in the least; in fact, their thoroughness and judgment made me feel safer as a traveler. I guess I happen to be an outlier in this world where political correctness and aversion to profiling outweighs common sense. What was it we learned as children? Oh yeah, safety first!

    Anyway, Amsterdam is behind me; so is Paris, and I'm heading home for the first time in a month. The droning of the flight, the wine, and the large comfortable seat has made me drowsy. I lay back, closed my eyes, and my mind tripped back to another time long ago, when I took another kind of journey, what the French call *reverie*…

***

Chapter 6: The Operation

The day began with a bright, almost cloudless azure sky. In the distance, I could see a great body of water, and over it, sea gulls, pelicans, and several other types of shorebirds were gliding gracefully, occasionally swooping down toward an unsuspecting fish. More often than not, they would seemingly change their minds in mid-descent and lift silently. Their shrill cries pierced an otherwise soundless morning.

I always thought it rained on days like this. As a child, growing up in northwest Ohio, I remember whenever there was a funeral in the family it rained. A morning drizzle always gave me a sense of foreboding, like it might be the day the guy with the scythe comes for me. Has to happen sooner or later. I prefer later. Yet where was the rain this day? Of course, I didn't really think the day would end with my funeral, but what I would be facing during the next several hours seemed almost as grim.

My head was spinning with thoughts of the infamous experiments conducted at Nazi prison camps like Buchenwald, where sterilization of both sexes was attempted by radiation. These thoughts made me slightly sick to my stomach as I tried to concentrate on the flight of the birds in the distance. But every time my body would start to relax, my eyes would involuntarily turn to the clock on the wall of the waiting room, and the knot in my stomach tightened. I empathized with the condemned man waiting his final hour. The helplessness of the situation made the frustration overpowering.

Doctor Tauzer had scheduled me to be brought before him at 9:30. I had dreaded this appointment for the past two years, when I first knew it was inevitable. In fact, since discovering the date and time of my destiny less than a week ago, sleep had virtually escaped me. At least the waiting was almost over. I could only hope that peace lay ahead.

As the hour grew close, I found myself becoming hopelessly paranoid. Things unknown to my conscious mind suddenly emerged from the subconscious. Things like new acquaintances asking me if I am Jewish. This had never seemed at all important to me until I started thinking of Buchenwald. My last name is also frequently mispronounced and misspelled "Mayer". In truth that is the actual spelling of my family name; actually Maijer, but in script i and j turns into y. Several generations ago, an ancestor changed the names of his children to Myers while leaving his own name unchanged. I once asked my Dad and uncles why. They didn't know. I was sure Doctor Tauzer and his staff made the same assumption. Soon they would discover I do not have the operation required of all Jewish males. Some victory. By then it wouldn't matter much.

It was 9:28 when I was taken to the building where Doctor Tauzer performed his duty. As I entered the anteroom, a large tough-looking woman dressed in white behind a massive wooden desk eyed me disapprovingly.

"Your name," she demanded curtly.

"Myers," I said.

"Ah, yes, Mr. Mayer…"

"Myers. M-Y-E-R-S," I corrected her.

"Mmm, yes, whatever.... We have been expecting you," she said with a cruel smile. "Fill out this form, please."

She handed me a sterile white paper with the usual questions on it: name, age, sex, etc., etc. Uh-oh, next of kin, notify in case of emergency. Why would they need to know that? Unless.... As I methodically filled out the form, attempting to draw out time, I couldn't help but wonder what was done with these records. Did they somehow use them to justify what they did? Pretending to study the form, I turned my eyes, being careful not to turn my head, toward the door. I weighed the odds. If I made a run for it, what was the chance of escape?

Chapter 6: The Operation

Realistically, of course, I realized it was nil. Eventually, I would just end up back in this wretched building.

When you are not in a situation like this, say watching a motion picture or television, it is easy to say you would attempt an escape. After all, you rationalize; at least you would have the satisfaction of knowing you tried. But, when you are *really* there, you look at it quite differently. Some call it fear; others call it shock; but in my case I believe it was ego. I was determined they would not see me as a sniveling coward begging for mercy, and to me at that time, running would be an admittance of cowardice. Also, my nerves were so highly strung that I was afraid I might go completely to pieces when returned to the evil Doctor Tauzer, as I knew I would be. I decided to face him like a "man," with courage and bravado. Inside I was coming apart. Trembling, I sat down and waited.

The moments weighed heavily on my mind. It had been five minutes since I sat down. Then ten. A ray of hope. Perhaps they had forgotten about me. Doubtful. But, maybe Doctor Tauzer was too busy or had been taken ill. That sounded more feasible, if improbable, but I clung to it. If I got a postponement, would I be as brave the next time? Stop worrying, I told myself, the operation may be cancelled. I mulled this over for a while, and had just started to relax when I realized about half a dozen other men had been brought into the anteroom and were sitting all about me.

I looked at each carefully. Searching. Wondering. Their countenances all had the hollow, blank stare of the doomed. I fleetingly wondered if I looked as bad, but knew the answer. As we glanced at each other, we felt a common bond. Several even smiled weakly. It was then I realized there would be no reprieve, no postponement, no cancellation, and that I was on the threshold of facing Doctor Tauzer's scalpel. Acceptance hit me like a thunderbolt. It was really happening! This was no child's nightmare, it was real. Nervous perspiration beaded on my brow, and trickled down the small of my back. I felt faint.

At 9:45, I caught a glimpse of a short, frail woman walking down the long hall from the examining and operating rooms. She was coming for us—for me! The closer she came, the more nauseous I became. When she entered the anteroom and whispered something to the tough-looking Wagnerian woman behind the desk, I observed she was fortyish with skin almost as white as her gown. It looked like one could poke his finger right through her flesh. The angel of death.

"Mr. Myers," boomed the big woman in a voice that gave me chills. This was it.

I looked up quizzically and the frail, little woman looked back sympathetically.

"We're ready for you now," she said quietly, but firmly. "Follow me please."

I stood up to test my wobbly legs, and steadied myself for the long walk down the corridor. The walk was not nearly as long as I hoped and anticipated, for she escorted me only as far as the first room on the left and gestured with her dainty hand for me to enter.

The room itself was very innocent looking. The walls and ceiling were painted an almost cheery yellow pastel. There was only room enough for a set of drawers along one wall, which was covered by a small counter. Above half of this array was a wall-mounted cabinet with a glass door that contained stoppered bottles with chemical symbols on them. Next to the opposite wall was a typical physician's examining cot. You know the kind they tell you to sit on while they probe your chest with a stethoscope. It was covered with tissue and had a small pillow at one end. Also along this wall, a doorway connected to another room.

Chapter 6: The Operation

I thought I heard activity from the adjoining room and, curious, started to move toward it. The frail, little woman stopped me with a surprisingly strong hand on my chest.

"Please drop your pants to your knees and lay back," she said, motioning me to the cot. (Aside: Now ordinarily a woman wouldn't have to ask twice, but in this situation, well....) Then, handing me a paper towel, she added, "You may cover yourself with this, if you wish."

Feeling very self-conscious, I complied with her command while she methodically arranged some instruments in a silver bowl, which she placed on a tray at the foot of the cot.

I didn't have to wait very long. Soon, a short, dark-haired man dressed in surgical scrubs bounded through the doorway from the adjacent room. His face was neither handsome nor homely, but he was severely marked, probably from a bad case of some kind of pox or childhood acne. He smiled and pumped my hand vigorously when he introduced himself, his eyes twinkling behind black, horn-rimmed glasses.

If his act was intended to relax me, it failed miserably. Now I wondered about his competency. Was this guy whacked out? I could feel the paper tissue covering the cot sticking to my perspiration-filmed arms and legs.

I couldn't take my eyes away from the silver bowl. Since I was lying down, the tray on which the bowl sat was above my eye level so I could not see the instruments themselves, just the varied configuration of their handles. Knives? Scissors? Pincers? I couldn't think of the medical names for them.

"Now just relax, Mr. Mayer...."

"Myers. M-Y-E-R-S," I said thickly. My mouth was exceptionally dry.

"... Mr. Myers, we'll have you finished in a jiffy," said Doctor Tauzer.

That's what I'm afraid of, I thought.

I saw a huge, and I mean gigantic, hypodermic needle in his hand moving toward my genital area, and I looked toward the ceiling waiting for indescribable pain. Strangely enough, none came.

***

"*Monsieur Myers, Monsieur Myers!*" It was a startled Air France flight attendant.

"*Oui, c'est moi,*" I said groggily still not fully alert.

She looked at me with concern.

I then realized I must have cried out in my sleep. "*Desolait, madame, de rien,*" I said embarrassed.

"*D'accord,*" she smiled and left. I fell back in my seat....

***

For what must have been hours, I laid there petrified and sweating profusely. Though I attempted to keep looking at the ceiling, my gaze kept involuntarily wandering down toward the surgeon's deftly moving hands. I felt no pain, only pressure. An occasional snipping sound played havoc with my imagination.

"Am I hurting you?" he said with some amusement, but behind his eyes I could hear a maniacal BWA-HA-HA-HA-HA!

"No," I replied quietly. "I don't know why I'm so tense. I suppose it's all in my head."

"I suppose," he said a bit bored and a bit too cool.

I shifted my eyes back to the ceiling and tried to think of something else. Anything. I tried to count the number of holes in the acoustical ceiling tiles. It was no use. Then suddenly the

Chapter 6: The Operation

faces of my wife and children appeared, and I thought of a summer past spent at the beach. Happy days. The children edging down to the water line, fascinated by the ebb and flow of the ocean. Running from the onrushing breakers, and laughing gleefully at the touch of the churning, cool sea water. The tender touch of my wife's hand upon my head as we watched. It seemed so long ago.

But wait... I no longer felt the pressure... or heard the snipping. Am I dead? Startled, I looked down and saw Doctor Tauzer's grinning face.

"We're all finished," he said. "You're free to go."

***

Somebody nudged me. "Hey, Gene," said a voice. "Buckle up; we're on final approach."

I cracked open my eyes. It was Nicole, who occupied the seat next to me. "Thanks," I yawned, and rubbed my eyes. I looked out the window and saw the Atascocita Country Club below, and thought of that day so long ago. I remembered the doctor leaving me alone....

***

However, before I left the room, Doctor Tauzer returned and handed me a small brass pin. He said it was for me being such a good patient. What, no lollipop?

When I gingerly walked back through the anteroom, the feeling of superiority over those not like me was overwhelming. It was certainly one of those rare times when I was tremendously pleased and proud of myself. I came through like a real trooper. Doctor Tauzer himself said I was a good patient, didn't he?

I glanced at the clock, and could scarcely believe what I saw. It was 10:00 *in the morning!* Just fifteen minutes had elapsed since the big, tough-looking woman called my name.

Strange, but now she didn't look so tough at all. She seemed soft and feminine. She smiled. "I'll bet you're glad *that's* over," she clucked. "Everything go all right?"

"Just great," I bubbled. "Didn't feel a thing."

"Don't forget to come back in two months," she said, waving as I left. I smiled and waved back my appointment card.

The southern California sun was warm and bright. It's reflection from the brass pin I held in my hand bobbed in my eyes and made me squint. An unusual pin to be sure. It was in the shape of the medical symbol for "male;" a circle with an arrow protruding from the upper right quadrant.

The only exception was that the circle was broken in one place, and a word was engraved on it.

Vasectomy.

Epilogue

My wife and I had discussed me getting the procedure for months, and I kept putting it off. But not for the reason you probably think; that is, most people assume it's a male ego type of thing connected to being made sterile. I didn't give a rat's ass about that. However, I greatly feared the dreaded "finger wave." I really did!

When a physician examines for prostate cancer, he sticks a gloved finger up your rectum and probes the gland checking for any abnormal growth. For me the feeling is very uncomfortable and creepy. With proper massage of the prostate, one can be made to ejaculate. That's what I heard they did at the two-month check up. Make sure you were shooting blanks so to speak.

Chapter 6: The Operation

So I came home for work one day, kissed my wife, and heard her say, "Oh, by the way, next Thursday you're going in for a vasectomy." She was so completely matter-of-fact it threw me even further off-balance.

"Huh? Wha…?" I felt slightly faint.

"Yeah, here's some reading material." She handed me a pamphlet.

I took it tentatively with shaking hands. "Hey, it says here I have to shave my scrotum! I have to prep myself? They gotta be kidding! What if I cut off my own nuts?"

She gave me an *"oh, well"* shrug, and said, "Well, you do what you have to do. Oh, and if you do cut them off, it'll save the need for an operation." She got a kick out of her attempt to make the situation humorous.

"Aw, come on! Where's the empathy? Where's the love?"

"Oh, don't be silly. And stop being such a baby."

Three days later I'm in the shower of the Manhattan Beach Athletic Club with a safety razor, and take a good look "down there." Damn things are as fuzzy as kiwis, except the hair is longer.

Okay. I can do this. Easy… easy…. Suddenly I'm aware of a half dozen or so grinning faces who, upon being discovered, start laughing like it's the funniest thing they've ever seen.

Later on Doctor Tauzer's operating table, he gave me this surprised look, "Why the hell did you do that?"

"Because it's in your pamphlet," I said, silently adding "dumb ass." I decided it wouldn't be in my best interest to get smart with some guy who is going to have a knife on and (gasp) *in* the family jewels.

"Oh," he chuckled. "That's an old pamphlet. We don't do that any more."

After the operation, he gave me some advice. "Okay, during the next two months I want you to get plenty of stick time so we get all those guys flushed out of there."

"Uh, okay." I'm thinking about the finger wave. He seemed to be reading my mind.

"Then on the day of your two-month appointment, get your wife to help you out, slap on a condom, and bring in the discharge."

"No finger wave?" I was ready to do hand-springs.

"No, no. It doesn't matter if they're alive or dead, just that there aren't any in there; otherwise the operation has failed."

Fast forward two months later. I woke up with massive morning wood. Damn thing seemed like it was made of blue steel. Couldn't hurt it with a hammer. I whipped on a waiting condom, woke up my wife, and was about to loudly proclaim, "I'm entering!"

Unfortunately, our four-year old daughter and one-year old son banged open the door, and entered our room on a dead run.

"What are you doing?" wondered our daughter.

"Nothing," I announced feebly, flopping on my back, woody gone forever.

Later in the doctor's office I sheepishly approached the desk and signed the appointment book.

The nurse looked up at me and smiled. "Do you have something for me?"

"Um...." My eyes are darting about, and I lick my dry lips.

"Maybe a sample," she said coyly, "In a used condom?"

"Uh, it didn't work out. I don't have my sample."

Chapter 6: The Operation

"Well, that's okay," she said, and handed me a glass beaker.

"What's this for?"

She smiled patiently. "I still need a sample, which we can get the easy way or the hard way."

"The easy way," I say pointing to the beaker, "Or the hard way, um, a finger wave?"

"That's right. There's a restroom right over there."

"Do you have any magazines or other kinds of aids?"

"Sorry. Just think of what you usually do."

I was in that restroom for forty-five minutes sweating bullets trying to get the job done. Masturbating for science. How cool is that? When I did think of a suitable fantasy, I remembered there were people on the outside who knew what I was doing in there.

I turned in an empty beaker.

I got a finger wave.

All turned out well, that is, the operation was a success, but why oh why didn't I simply cancel the appointment and make another?

Chapter 7

Germs, Contamination, and Disease

WARNING: This chapter contains graphic material, which some may find distasteful.

FRANKFORT WAS a three-hour stopover on my way from Riyadh to Houston. I intentionally skipped breakfast, and only partook of some Moroccan tea and two or three dates on the Saudi Arabian Airlines flight. By the time I arrived at the Lufthansa international departure concourse I was famished. The business and first class lounge, as usual, was well supplied with food and beverages, so I loaded a plate, grabbed a beer, and found a stool at the bar. While dining alone I prefer a bar to a dining room mainly for the benefit of conversation with the bartenders, drink runners, and other bar sitters.

I noticed the fellow on my left was rather greedily gulping scotch whiskey in contrast to the beers the rest of us were

Chapter 7: Germs, Contamination, and Disease

sipping. He looked like a businessman, but was a bit unkempt; that is, his clothes fit well and were expensive, but a bit worn, as were the air-vented wing-tips on his feet. He was about mid-forty with just the hint of a paunch. Well-groomed, but his salt-and-pepper hair was slightly shaggy.

I caught his eye and tipped my beer toward his whiskey. "Breakfast of champions?"

"A bit of a celebration," he replied, taking a long pull and indicating to the bartender to top up his glass. He exhaled loudly and gave me a self-satisfied look. We introduced ourselves. His name was Richard something.

"Congratulations on having something to celebrate," I offered.

"Thanks." He looked at me thoughtfully. "Tell me something, my friend, have you ever been considered to have no value? I mean, you know, worked for a firm for years… moving up the org chart… then when it's your turn, you get what they now call downsized?"

"Because you're making too much, receiving bonuses, getting too old maybe?"

"Yeah, except for the too old part. Gotta be late fifties for that to kick in."

"I usually get fired for being insubordinate," I said, only half-joking.

"Well, I've been downsized, or in my case out-and-out screwed, twice in the last ten years, but not before I did some major damage to their customer service systems as a parting shot." He sat back and grinned. "Didn't know what hit 'em, and I was always such a serious, dyed-in-the-wool company man… you know, all business all the time… that I was the last person in the world they'd suspect to be a saboteur." He laughed heartily and ended with a slight coughing jag.

"Neither ever contacted you after the fact to see what happened?"

"Oh, hell yeah. Both of 'em. Paid me consulting fees to find the problems and fix them...." He started the laughing, coughing jag again. "But I still left a few surprises to kick in later."

"Yeah, I get it. Give 'em a chance to bring you back again, right?" I decided the guy had no integrity.

"Well, that was the master plan, but it didn't work out. Must've figured it out on their own. Bastards."

"It's been tough for management and executives to find work these days. You ever hook up with anyone after that?"

"Nope. Had to survive on my own, and it's been a bitch. Failed marriage, apartment living, ten-year-old car, borrowing money to get by, until...." He looked down at the bar, smiled widely, shook his head, and took a drink of the whiskey.

"But you're celebrating...." I began.

"Damn right. Just sold a couple forty-foot containers of gas masks to this big cheese Arab sheikh in Dubai. My take is just over three million US." He sat back beaming to let his words take effect then broke into another loud round of laughing and coughing.

"Wow, good for you. I guess that's the best way to get even." I raised my beer to him in mock appreciation for his accomplishment, but there was something really "off" about him. In addition to what I considered an integrity issue there was something else; an inherent feeling that made me want to get away from this guy. I couldn't imagine being trapped on an airplane next to him for any amount of time.

"I'll do more than that," he said with a kind of sly, sideways look. "You see, I like to mess with people."

Chapter 7: Germs, Contamination, and Disease

Then he related the twelve-year-old story that follows. As a warning to the reader, the following material is graphic and vulgar; however, keep in mind my goal is to report unusual things that happened to me outside regular business hours during my travels.

***

Richie sat on a barstool at the Fox Sports Skybox overlooking Gate E16 at Houston's Bush Intercontinental Airport, or simply, IAH. To a casual on-looker he appeared to be the archetype of a serious young businessman. He was fit and trim, well-groomed, dressed in a gray pinstriped, three-button suit with a crisp blue button-down shirt and a club tie. His black leather computer case occupied the stool next to him.

But serious? No way. Everything seemed darkly amusing to him. It was a secret, snide form of humor that occurred behind people's backs, and was practiced mostly—but not entirely—among strangers. His business underlings, peers, and superiors thought him to be a dry, stoic, humorless kind of guy. Nose to the grindstone. Dedicated to the company's success. No one ever thought the continuous, unsolved, irritating pranks at the office—graphite on handles of desk drawers, insects in the refrigerator, salt in the water cooler, a dead fish taped under a desk, dog poop in the microwave, boogers wiped on telephone handles—had anything to do with Richie. Actually, he was Richard to his co-workers. His "Captain Chaos" alter ego, Richie, was his secret alone.

For Richie, entertainment was to be found voyeuristically, especially if it caused discomfort to someone else. I'm sure you know the type. Kind of like the arsonist that stays around to watch others struggle with what he has done.

Richie's flight to Cleveland didn't leave for another two hours.

"May as well get a little buzz on," he thought out loud, and pondered whether to order a Martini or Manhattan. This was a dubious decision, Richie not having much tolerance for alcohol, especially the hard stuff. Over the bar, nine television screens flickered silently while hits from the 70s and 80s filled the room at a volume one notch too high. On the TV screens were shows featuring an NFL rerun, called curiously, *NFL Live*, the Weather Channel, a nine-ball billiards match, and a show called *Coast2Coast* trying to build excitement for women's basketball, possibly the most boring and least watched sport on the planet.

He hailed the bartender, a kid with a round peach fuzz face, and ordered a Manhattan straight up with Maker's Mark bourbon. The kid pulled down a martini glass and shaker, a good start, and then asked, "You don't want any sweet vermouth?"

"Yes, of course."

"You said straight."

"I said straight up, which means in a martini glass." Geez, what a maroon. Richie wondered what the kid would have said had he ordered a perfect Manhattan. Damned bartenders these days don't know how to mix anything. Order a Martini and they ask if you want vodka or gin. A Martini is always gin. Otherwise, you order a *vodka* Martini, dumb ass. Mainly, they just pour beer and wine or margaritas out of a slush machine. Sometimes they even screw that up. Here's an example: A cute, young waitress in Philadelphia last week thought all white wines were called Chardonnay.

"I asked for Sauvignon Blanc," said Richie.

"Yes. That's just another type of Chardonnay," said the waitress in a tone that implied Richie was ignorant.

Chapter 7: Germs, Contamination, and Disease

They got into a mild argument, neither giving in, but Richie called it off just before both reached a point of anger having surmised how to turn the situation to his advantage. Pretty soon they started having this little running joke with each other, both thinking the other was wrong, but in a fun and flirtatious kind of way. He had a talent for getting stuff like that started. Better yet, he took her home (her place) and enjoyed some great bedroom aerobics. Richie also took her slumbering, bare-ass picture with his cell phone and posted it with her phone number on the internet with one of those "for a good time call..." tag lines. Hey, it was true! She was a good time, just didn't know shit about wine.

He looked around the Skybox and saw a number of people who looked like him, but more who wore "business casual" attire, and one table full of young men with jeans and baseball caps. Most of the solitary customers (those with bored expressions) were tapping on their laptop computers. The only females were waitresses. There was this one old fart, several stools from him, drinking some kind of whiskey on the rocks, but everyone else was drinking beer. You could tell he was from an earlier generation, wearing a tie with a short sleeve shirt and no coat. The shirt always gave them away; began their careers before the advent of office air-conditioning.

Manhattan tasted good. He ordered another, and mainly for something to do, studied the bar menu. It was either that or fart around with his notebook; that's what Dell preferred to call his laptop. Caesar salad with grilled chicken looked good. Hadn't eaten since breakfast. Richie finished his second Manhattan and ordered the Caesar with a glass of Shiraz. The wine came at once, and he polished it off quickly while studying passing ladies with emphasis on their derrières, compiling a mental "to do" list, as in I'd "do" that one.

A nice buzz was beginning complete with giddiness. Might as well have another Shiraz. After still another glass, the salad finally showed up, which was a spicy Buffalo chicken salad instead of the Caesar. No matter. He wondered about it before ordering the Caesar and welcomed the mistake. It was indeed spicy, but tasty, and guaranteed to give him world class halitosis for sure. Oh well, maybe the alcohol would offset it. Better have a glass of brandy—make it a double.

Richie eavesdropped on a debate between the young bartender and an equally young waitress about rock concerts. She gave the appearance of having a bad attitude about life. Her upper lip arched over her front teeth exposing them and her braces. She resembled Butthead from the old *Beavis and Butthead* cartoons. Looked like a car grill; maybe a '57 Buick.

When Richie finally left the Skybox for nearby Gate E17, he was feeling no pain. This always made everything seem even more humorous. The salad, or something, gave him an inexhaustible source of flatulence. It came out frequently in a hot, silent rush with a kind of whoosh sound. He could feel his sphincter burn, and whoa, what a sauerkraut shithouse of a smell! It made him chortle as he moved around the area evacuating the intestinal vapor. People would, "Oh, my God!" and look disapprovingly at some sloppily dressed, unkempt young man sitting nearby.

This was by design. Richie knew no one ever suspected a woman or a guy dressed in a neatly pressed suit. After he gassed each area, he moved off and tittered until tears streamed from his eyes. The expressions of the victims inhaling the gag-inducing, foul stench were priceless. Richie wondered if any air borne particles accompanied the fumes. The thought of someone actually ingesting some ass matter was even funnier. He hid behind a column out of sight of the affected area, and laughed until he damn near collapsed.

He couldn't wait to board his flight figuring any slumbering male form nearby, always a sure thing, would receive the blame. Meanwhile, he, Richie, would be seriously working on

Chapter 7: Germs, Contamination, and Disease

his notebook ready to wrinkle up his nose and give a wide-eyed "what the hell?" look while subtly pointing out a sleeping passenger to others holding their breath and nose. What kick-ass fun!

He made a mental note to check his shorts when he got home. Might even have to wrap them in tinfoil and jettison them. Had he known in advance that his bowels would be so active, he could have gone "commando" and cut out a layer of filtering. After the thought occurred, Richie retired to the restroom to remove his underwear, but after carefully considering the probability of getting shit stains on his suit trousers changed his mind. Hey, cheaper to toss a pair of shorts than dry clean slacks, y'know?

Predictably, the flight to Cleveland was two and a half hours of nonstop nauseating odors, which Richie fueled by drinking beer and chomping peanuts. At one point he called a flight attendant over and suggested the sleeping guy in the row ahead of him across the aisle may have soiled himself. A lady in the window seat, separated by an empty seat from Richie, seconded the motion.

"My God, it's awful!" agreed the attendant.

"Isn't there something you can do?" asked the window seat lady.

Richie gave the attendant a hopeful nod with pleading eyes.

Inside he was coming apart barely able to contain himself. "Maybe you should wake him. See if he's all right." Richie said this with tears in his eyes and stifled a giggle quickly covering with a serious face.

"Yes, please!" roared an immaculately dressed man in the seat directly behind Richie. The guy had big-time, expensive, obnoxious, holier-than-thou, rich lawyer written all over him.

"I have a very important client meeting me, and it won't do if I smell like a pig sty!"

"Well, okay," said the attendant uncomfortably. She shook the sleeper gently. He was a pimply-faced, twenty-something lard-ass with greasy hair that needed cut, and rumpled clothes that needed laundering. A perfect foil for Richie.

He awoke with a start and made a face. Looked like he hadn't brushed his teeth in a month, like he was eating pea soup.

"Are you all right, sir?" The attendant backed off a little, a reaction to the guy's BO. Richie thought it was perfect, as in, what a perfect fall guy.

The fall guy scrunched up his eyes and grimaced some more. "Hey, what's that rotten smell? Who shit?" he said too loudly. The attendant's face reddened. Richie was losing it, putting a pillow over his face so his uncontained laughing looked like misery.

"You did, lout! Please get control of yourself, you obnoxious lummox!" said the lawyer with irritation and impatience. "Maybe you should go to the bathroom, and stay there! For God's sake have some consideration for those around you!"

"Hey, fuck you, asswipe! It's not me! Besides, who ever smelt it, dealt it." He looked around and grinned like he'd come up with a good one.

"Oh, I'm *so* sure," Richie whispered to the lady in his row who rolled her eyes and fanned the air with a magazine. Richie dived back into the pillow, his body shaking uncontrollably. Maybe he could instigate a fistfight.

Finally, everything returned to normal; that is, the fall guy went back to sleep after which Richie loosed a continuous hot stream of rotten, intestinal zephyr that seemed to grow more and more sour and putrid. The staying power was incredible,

Chapter 7: Germs, Contamination, and Disease

what a fart connoisseur would call "hangers." Now, passengers rows away were showing annoyance. Richie had another beer and opened his vent jet to full-on to blast the odor away from him. Many others followed suit. This, of course, made things worse by spreading the stench even further throughout the aircraft.

The lawyer continued to complain loudly throughout the flight. The flight attendants seemed helpless, which exacerbated his anger.

When Richie followed the fall guy up the aisle as they were deplaning, he continued to issue silent-but-deadly gas while turning around, shaking his head with disbelief and irritation, and pointing to the poor sap ahead of him.

"This plane smells like shit," the fall guy said to two flight attendants buh-bying everyone. He also let loose a juicy sneeze into his hand, which he wiped on his jeans. "I may sue this flying shithouse for causing me allergies."

"Yes, thanks to you and your rudeness, you asinine slob!" said the snooty, lawyer-type behind Richie.

"Maybe it's his breath," Richie whispered over his shoulder while whooshing off another one. Come on fist fight.

"Maybe it's your breath!" said the lawyer loudly.

"Don't blame your problems on me!" the kid retorted. "Probably a combination of your rotten shorts and that shitty, faggy cologne you wear! Stuff's so bad it even overpowers your farts!"

The lawyer, red-faced because he had been wrongly accused, blustered with anger and cursing, but couldn't manage a suitable comeback other than "You, you... you uncouth oaf."

"Oh yeah, homo? I'm gonna kick your ass when we get outside!"

"You just try it," hissed the lawyer. Richie thought he was the kind of guy who'd have his underlings hold the poor sap while he pounded on him. Passengers looked back and forth, some maybe wondering who to blame, but still, the choice seemed obvious. People were practically trampling each other to get off the airplane.

Richie felt light-headed and giddy, and had a hard time walking without concentrating thanks to the combination of mirth and too much alcohol. He also had a difficult time controlling additional emissions that were now starting to become quite loud. Fortunately, typical air terminal commotion provided cover for the noise.

At the baggage claim area, the lawyer sat off by himself, leaving an underling to retrieve his bag. The junior associate clustered with others around the carrousel. Richie, with only a carry-on, reeled by and lost his balance as he neared the lawyer. He fell awkwardly smack into the lap of the astonished barrister while expelling a rumbling blast that vibrated the poor guy's body from shoulder to thigh as Richie's buttocks worked its way down, ripping off a button and slightly tearing a lapel. The odor was overpowering and immediate.

"Son of a fucking bitch!" yelled the lawyer, but nobody paid heed, their attention on the rotating carrousel.

"Sorry," giggled Richie his face scarcely an inch from the face of his victim. He also involuntarily let go with a volcano-like, rattling belch that smelled like rancid puke.

"Oh geez!" the lawyer gagged, trying not to vomit, and Richie let fly with a juicy, mucus-filled sneeze. They guy's face was splattered with snot.

Before the lawyer could react, Richie straightened himself by pushing off on the guy's formerly neatly combed hair and pulling himself up by his necktie, restricting his throat and temporarily disabling his ability to speak. Richie, heel on the lawyer's foot, also shit his pants when he stood, part of a mushy turd rolling down his leg and depositing itself on the lawyer's shoe.

Richie staggered toward the door.

The sleepy-looking fall guy turned around from the carrousel, pointed at the lawyer, and yelled, "See, I told you it was that asshole!"

Everyone looked, obviously disgusted, and shook their heads.

Chapter 8

The Kingdom

I ARRIVED in Riyadh from Paris about six in the afternoon on Sunday, July 1. It was our wedding anniversary, and I missed Kay who, always the trooper, had not complained about my self-centered nature when we parted. She never did. But, truth to tell, I was lonely and felt the sting of sorrow and regret.

Touraj was supposed to have arranged for someone from the local office of Amkest to greet my arrival, but after Saudi Arabian Customs released me—after completely unpacking and dismantling my luggage—it was clear I was on my own. This was the first lesson that Touraj could not be depended upon for anything, no matter how inconsequential. To do so would result in disappointment and anger. It was also an omen about the future of our business enterprise.

On the positive side, I met a Pakistani gentleman, Asif Mirza, in the customs line, who became an almost daily tennis partner. Like me, Asif had left his wife and young children behind; in his case, for at least six months. Also, like me, he experienced the heavy hand of remorse.

Chapter 8: The Kingdom

Nevertheless, no matter how positive I tried to be, a strong feeling of exasperation prevailed. It seemed like I had been on the plane forever. I was tired, in a strange land, and scheduled to be separated from Kay for four months. I had no idea where to go, but being a seasoned international traveler, wasn't overly concerned, just royally pissed off. Fortunately, I still had the business card the Amkest chairman, Amr Khashoggi, gave me in Newport Beach.

Since Sunday is a normal workday in the Middle East, and businesses are open until seven or eight in the evening, I knew I would catch someone at the office.

"Amkest International," answered a male voice. His accent was Urdu.

"*Salaam Aleikum*," I said, using the preferred Islamic greeting, peace be with you.

"*Waleikum esalaam*," and upon you, peace, said the voice.

The business language throughout the Middle East is English so I switched tongues.

"May I speak to Sheikh Amr?"

"He is not here. He has gone home."

After further conversation, I learned that the voice was Sethu (say-toe) from India, who was Amr's secretary. No one had informed him, or anyone else, I would be arriving, even though the trip had been set up weeks before. I made a mental note to cuss out Touraj with gusto, and get into a greasy, black funk of a mood before I did so. That wouldn't be difficult. Sethu suggested I take a taxi to a hotel, and call the office about ten the next morning. He'd send a car for me.

The Al Khozama Hotel in central Riyadh was bustling when I arrived. A cocktail would have been nice, but I would be without libation for the next four months, that being the rule of the land. To be caught with alcohol (or pork products) was to be flogged publicly, jailed for six months, and deported, although it was said to be a challenge to stay alive that long in a Saudi jail. The entire hotel staff was male, mostly from the Indian peninsula, the Philippines, or Indo-China.

Later I discovered that women were not allowed to work except as physicians or educators. Of the seventeen million people in the Kingdom of Saudi Arabia, seven million are expats hired to be construction and factory workers, taxi and bus drivers, hotel personnel, etc. The unemployment rate is a staggering twenty-five percent, but is because of preference, not lack of jobs. The Bedouins still prefer to live a nomadic lifestyle.

Another Indian, Thomas, himself a Christian, collected me the following morning for the trip to the office. On the way, we passed a bombed out apartment complex where a number of US servicemen had lost their lives. The perpetrators, all Saudis, had been caught and beheaded, according to Thomas. He said this was over the objections of the US Government who demanded custody of the bombers so they could be put on trial. Thomas smiled, shook his head, and looked at me.

"Is your country so broken that everything revolves around lawyers?" he wondered. "Can not they see our law is more just and swift, and a better economic solution?"

"Some parts of Islam refer to my country as the great Satan," I answered. "And in some ways they are right. We are full of self-promotion, think we're better than everyone else, and our god is money. Truth to tell, we're not much more than a pretty girl with the clap." Here, I secretly got a kick out of my metaphor, then said, "But that's what you see on the outside. Underneath we're a decent, caring people deeply concerned about our fellow man."

Chapter 8: The Kingdom

Thomas nodded and thought in silence for a while. Several weeks prior to my arrival, another more serious bombing took place in the Dammam, Dharhan, and Jubail area. More than twenty US Marines lost their lives in the Khobar Towers.

Thomas said they hadn't caught those bombers yet. He suggested that I not let on that I'm American; maybe pretend that I'm from somewhere else. Besides, he said, I don't look or act American. That threw me.

"How can you say that?" I asked.

"Oh, you can tell where everyone is from because of their features," he explained.

"But Americans are from everywhere else," I answered. "I doubt that even the people we call Native Americans are originally from there." At least that's what the Mormons say, but I didn't mention that.

"You look English," Thomas said.

"How do Brits and Americans differ in appearance?"

"Americans have longer faces and heads," Thomas said as though explaining to a child.

"Oh." Not knowing how or caring to continue this strange conversation; I stared out the window in silence for the rest of the ride.

Amr was animatedly and thoroughly chewing out Sethu (Amr called him C-2) about something when I arrived with Thomas. Later, I observed the same phenomenon about twice a day every day, often with Sethu being fired and re-hired within the hour. Sethu was clueless about office politics, discretion, and Amr's ego when it came to reminding his boss about minor mistakes or something Amr may have done or said wrongly. Arabs do not like to be reminded about errors (who does?), and Sethu would not back off. It was like he was constantly picking a scab. One of Amr's vice presidents from Lebanon, Samer Cha'ar, always referred to Sethu disparagingly and sneeringly as Igor—right to his face! Sethu remained unfazed.

Amr ushered me into his office. "I didn't know you were arriving today, but welcome."

"Touraj was supposed to have called two days ago. I normally take care of something like that myself, but he insisted," I replied. In a land where form is everything, this was a major faux pas. I cursed Touraj again under my breath.

"Well, no matter," smiled Amr. "You're here."

It took me awhile to get used to seeing him in the *thobe* and *ghutra* traditional dress of a Saudi. When I met him in the US, he wore western dress and looked European to me, but then again, I can't tell features! As I later got to know Amr intimately, I discovered he was a chameleon. He spoke Arabic, Spanish, French, and English without a flaw. People seemed immediately charmed by him because of his handsome appearance, outgoing personality, and his uncanny ability to know all the little nuances of whatever language he was speaking, including the idioms and jokes of the particular area as well. Frankly, the guy amazed me. He was also the president of the Young Presidents Organization (YPO) for the Gulf Coast Community (GCC), which is basically the Arabian Peninsula, and Austral-Asia. The guy was connected.

Amr's older brother, Adnan, was considered the richest man in the world back in the 1980s. At that time he was doing a lot of building around Salt Lake City. Then somehow he got crosswise with the government, and stood trial in New York City with Imelda Marcos for something. I think he skipped the country, but years later I saw him front and center on television during the funeral of Richard Nixon.

Chapter 8: The Kingdom

We decided my first bit of business would be for me to fly to Dharhan the next day and meet with executives, managers, and engineers of Yusuf Bin Achmed Kanoo, a large international shipping company, among other things. After a quick phone call by Amr, it was arranged. The chairman was one of Amr's buddies. We wanted Kanoo to try an industrial lubricant we made in Florida for their factory machinery, work vehicles, and ocean-going vessels. Amr had already given his friend a sample to try in his firearms, and the guy loved it. Suddenly, Amr looked at me with concern.

"Have you had tea yet?"

"No." I didn't know I was supposed to.

"C-2, come!!!" he thundered.

As the rest of the day passed, I became acquainted with Amkest office personnel, most of whom were computer science-types, engineers and accountants from Lebanon, India, Sudan, and Egypt. Mohammed Gad, a Sudanese engineer, asked me if I could tell his national origin. This seemed to be a game among them.

"I don't know; India?" I ventured.

"No!" he replied with exasperation, "I'm from Sudan! Can't you tell from my features?"

"No."

More exasperation. "You can tell where everybody's from by their features!"

Upon returning to the Al Khozama Hotel, I checked out and moved to a suite in the Al Khozama Center, which was adjacent to the hotel and owned by the same people. Therefore, I retained rights to the hotel restaurants and swimming pool. The Al Khozama Center was a fourteen-story building with businesses on the first two levels—restaurants, delicatessen, dry cleaner, travel agency, art galleries, etc.—apartments from levels three to thirteen, and a first-class athletic club on fourteen. The roof also had basketball and tennis courts. My fifth floor apartment was new, spacious, completely equipped, and tastefully furnished. It had a large balcony overlooking the hotel on one side and a large mosque on the other.

Although I flew frequently between Riyadh to either Dharhan on the Persian Gulf or Jeddah on the Red Sea, my residence in Riyadh was ideal. Business hours were 8:00 to 1:00, a three-hour break, and 4:00 to 7:00. The weekend consisted of one-half day on Friday and all day Saturday. I used "siesta time" and weekends to workout at the athletic club or swim laps at the pool. After hours before dinner, I played basketball with the Saudis or tennis with Asif Mirza. It wasn't home by a long shot, but tolerable.

The following day, my first *real* business day in KSA, I departed for Dharhan. I was one of a few westerners descending from the cabin of a massive, wheezing, old Lockheed L-1011 operated by Saudi Arabian Airlines. The steps were mounted on a truck and must have been three stories high. The desert heat of Riyadh was joined by the humidity of the Persian Gulf. Oppressive? You bet. Houston felt arid by comparison. I was not looking forward to a climb back up those steps later in the day.

A Kanoo senior manager and one of his staff greeted me coolly. I later found out they already had a full day planned when the CEO told the manager to give me his entire department's full attention instead. I was just another pushy American. This was not the start I preferred.

Later, I had lunch at an outdoor café with a young Kanoo application engineer. From my seat I had a view of the bombed out Khobar Towers. What a day. Could it get much worse?

Chapter 9

After Hours in KSA

WARNING: *This chapter contains material that may be offensive to those with an aversion to bidets.*

I'VE WRITTEN *this chapter in present tense so the reader will share this experience with me in the moment. My options of after hours entertainment were severely limited in Riyadh. Whenever I'm in this type of environment, my mind tends to wander mostly from boredom, which often results in me seeing everyday objects or events with "new eyes." This is one such occasion.*

One month down and business is proceeding well enough to merit a bit of optimism. A young Saudi in the Riyadh office, Rajeeb Rajab Al-Malki, decided to "adopt" me. I'm not sure exactly why, but I suspect he and Amr have been conspiring to convert me to Islam. My Arabic and his English are both too deficient to allow a great deal of conversation, but we manage. Rajeeb and Amr have also given me a name, Abu Jaafar, meaning father of Geoffrey, which is indeed the name of my son. On occasion, Rajeeb corrupts this new name somewhat by calling me Abu Geof. Rajeeb is short of stature but looks like one of

Chapter 9: After Hours in KSA

those Hollywood-depicted, wild-eyed Arab revolutionaries of Allah, riding a horse across the desert at breakneck speed waving a sword.

Rajeeb's main duty is to interface for Amkest with Saudi government officials. Amkest is Amr Mohamed Khashoggi's company headquartered in Riyadh with offices in Jeddah. It is a holding corporation for four separate and unrelated businesses: 1) selling and servicing computer hardware and software throughout the Kingdom of Saudi Arabia, 2) a trucking fleet to ship goods throughout the Kingdom, 3) making portion packs for Saudi Arabian Airlines, and 4) selling vehicles to the KSA government. I have an office courtesy of Amr who I met in Newport Beach, California months before.

Two or three times a week, Rajeeb swings by my apartment about ten in the evening to collect me for a thirty-minute trip into the desert, where the nights are peaceful, balmy, and starlit. The destination is a beautiful open air site on the sand complete with padded carpets and tents, which is owned by Rajeeb and his buddies mostly military officers, princes, and government officials.

By the way, any male born to a prince is also a prince, and given that most of them have between twenty and forty offspring, princes are legion. It is said there are twelve thousand princes in the Kingdom, of which nine thousand live in Riyadh. Each receives a monthly stipend from the government equivalent to nine thousand US dollars. Not a bad allowance. The teen-aged royals cavort about in their Rolls-Royces and Bentleys, yelling out the windows and generally acting out in the type of behavior typical of spoiled, entitled children. Hey, it's the human condition when home training is absent.

Back to the dessert: All males wear traditional Arab dress of *ghuttra* and *thobe*. (In that respect you cannot tell rich from poor except the former have their garments dry-cleaned and wear fragrant cologne.) There is also a Pakistani cook. Usually, we play cards and drink tea until midnight when we eat a meal of *kubsah*, then hang around shooting the breeze until almost daybreak. Rajeeb delivers me back to my apartment before sounding of *azan* for Morning Prayer.

I may as well admit it: I get bored. I mean, I am a member of a very well equipped athletic club located on the top two stories of my apartment building, but one can only indulge in so much tennis and squash racquets, treadmill running, lap swimming, and weight training. And anyway, I do most of that during the three-hour afternoon break. Television is censored and limited mainly to cricket ties from India, religious programs, and old movies in French or Arabic. There are no movie houses, theaters, or night spots because mixing of male and female is only allowed in a mosque, and quite restricted there. Given the Spartan conditions, my idle brain wanders into new territory; often some type of bizarre-o world.

With that in mind, there are two things on my mind worthy of discussion in this chapter. The first is that I think I may have been the only non-smoker in the Kingdom. Really! The Saudis think it is very odd that I do not smoke. Rajeeb, with a look of incredulity on his face, asked, "Abu Jaafar, why you not smoke?"

I couldn't think of an answer that would make sense to him, so I said, "It hurts my lungs."

"Oh." He seemed satisfied with my answer.

"How much do you smoke, Rajeeb?"

"Four box a day," (meaning four packs of Marlboros) he said proudly.

Even at the athletic club, everyone smokes. They run on the treadmill or climb the Stairmaster for up to an hour. Then they may play squash racquets or take an aerobics class. Afterward, they're all sitting in the juice bar/café area smoking up a

Chapter 9: After Hours in KSA

storm. For people who won't touch alcohol and pork products (both illegal) because the Prophet said they were unhealthy and banned by God, the tobacco habit is strangely inconsistent. Then again, they didn't have cigarettes in Mohammed's day. There are no areas anywhere in KSA designated as No Smoking.

My second discussion item is the presence of bidets in most bathrooms. I didn't think much about it at first because in many bathrooms of the world, especially Europe, bidets are ubiquitous. But then I started wondering, why are bidets in all-male athletic clubs toilets and office building toilets? If you're wondering, only males work in offices. There are no ladies rooms. I connected this wonderment to several other facts I observed, to wit:

- KSA toilet paper rolls only contain 25 to 30 percent of the amount of paper of a US roll, and

- In some Islamic counties the toilet is a hole in the ground at floor level that one either stands or squats over (there are guides showing where your feet go) depending on what you have to do. A military pilot friend of mine, not knowing how to squat properly, once deposited a septic log right into his dropped trousers. He said from then on he simply removed all his clothes.

- Many toilets, hole-in-the-ground or standard "throne," feature a yucky, corroded, grubby hose dangling alongside. Toilet paper may or may not be available.

- Ablutions (cleaning) must only be done with the left hand.

Eureka! "Ablutions" means butt-cleaning, sphincter douching, colon cleansing, ass flushing, poop-shoot pressure-washing, junk-in-the-trunk hosing, bung-hole bathing, rectum reaming, whatever. Those aren't bidets (per se), they're butt washers! Their function is the same as the grubby hoses. And when toilet paper is available, it's for left-handed butt drying! So, what the hell, in my apartment I tried it. Commode and bidet were side-by-side. I mean to tell you after that experiment, wiping with paper (rather coarse at that) left-handed, and trying to hop from one station to the next, without losing something in between, was quite a challenge. I wasn't sure whether or not you wipe before or after the hose-down so I did it on both ends. For those sites with only a hose, well, you know... hope the water pressure is good. Managing the operation with the clothes the natives wear must be a son-of-a-gun during ablutions. First of all, *thobes* hang to the ground, which would be like trying to deal with a three-foot long shirt tail while trying to take a dump then douche your sphincter. Now there's a great scene to visualize. Imagine one attempting to hop from one porcelain throne to another while holding a humongous bundle of cloth—white cloth at that! Usually, they wear white pants beneath the *thobe*. So, let's see, you'd have a guy with underwear (hopefully), and pants around his ankles holding up this humongous shirt-tail while negotiating from one station to another. And trying not to drip; i.e., keeping the sphincter puckered.

The bidet/butt-washers have hot and cold water faucets so the temperature and the pressure can be varied according to one's pleasure. Wow! Hydraulic corn-holing. Too much pressure could results in an unwanted or unintended enema, couldn't it? Too much temperature could result in an unintentional hemorrhoid operation. Man-oh-man, I just cauterized those babies! I can imagine a limp-wristed, sissified "flamer" with such an appliance. Getting off at both ends simultaneously.

Chapter 9: After Hours in KSA

Imagine an authority figure twisting the handle of the locked bathroom door. "I've been hearing that water running for a long time now. What's going on in there?"

Breathless response: "I-I'll be out in just a minute." (Beads of sweat on forehead from seeing the doorknob turn, and unsure if the door is locked. *Did I or didn't I?*)

And another thing: Although the bidets look like a commode, there is a normally open metal plug in the bottom. Like in your lavatory or bathtub. Located on top of the bidet with the hot and cold water taps is a lever to close the plug. What's the thinking here? Do they think someone would actually like to collect or save the water after butt cleaning? For crying out loud, *who*?! For what purpose? Excuse me sir, I must have this ass water analyzed.

My pondering was interrupted by *Meghreb Salat*, or the fourth prayer of the day. I turned on the television to watch the faithful enter the Prophet's Mosque in Medina, and thought no more about ablutions. But, hey, I really felt clean.

Chapter 10

The Last Cult

THROUGHOUT MY career I have been perplexed by our human condition. One would think that sooner or later I would catch on. I don't. I find myself caught by surprise at every turn. We are a paradox: vindictive and forgiving; selfless and selfish all at the same time. In this chapter I cite two examples. The first features a diverse collection of ruthless self-centered partners each out for personal interests at the expense of the success of the whole; the second is a group of "nice" people with a team first attitude, but also with a serious human flaw.

I arrived home from Saudi Arabia just before Christmas, and had no intention of returning to the Kingdom. Over the previous eleven months a very promising business venture had gone south and was irreparable, though at the time I wasn't willing to admit it. My role was to be the conduit among an unlikely cast of diverse, international, ego-centric characters for the purpose of fashioning a can-do, energized, profitable business team. In the end I failed, unable to cope with what seemed like increasing degrees of greed-driven autism; a year of my life down the drain. Mostly I blamed Touraj, the Iranian

Chapter 10: The Last Cult

from Newport Beach that got me into the venture in the first place; and it was also he who became the major architect behind all the divisive personality cock-ups.

The product itself was outstanding, a metal-conditioning chemical, endorsed by NASA, that would significantly enhance any application using oil for a lubricant. NASA used it on the Space Crawler, the monstrosity that carries the Space Shuttle to the launch pad. They also provided us with invaluable test data conducted by their own laboratories.

Thinking back, maybe a major omen of how events would unfold was the composition of the team. I'll start with the inventor. The guy was an absolute screwball. He believed the government was after him, and would only talk from public telephones or meet you at some out-of-the-way place at a weird hour. According to him, he'd been incarcerated at a hidden away federal prison, and sprung through the work of some legal genius who "had" something on the feds. We met that guy as well. What a maroon! Said he had this whole team of MBAs working for him, but the guy himself had trouble stringing two sentences together; plus, he looked like a nut. Wore two different shoes, had his shirt half hanging out, and unkempt hair like Bozo the Clown. He also had a blond bimbo selling stuff out of the back of his car to passers-by and nearby hotel residents.

The inventor was represented by a chemical company in Florida, the owner, Buck, more interested in auto racing than his firm. Oddly, he and the inventor loathed each other. In addition, mistrust ran deep among the people in the firm, each bad-mouthing the others to outside people like me. The metal-conditioning chemical was made there. A mysterious fire destroyed a new factory not six months old, and now they occupied an ancient but adequate building. The inventor was suspected as the torch, but proof was never found.

Newport Beach entrepreneurs, Touraj and Barry, had a relationship with the Khashoggi family in Saudi Arabia. Amr, the younger brother, tried the product and was astounded at its performance. He made a deal with Touraj and Barry to exclusively market the product throughout the Middle East, Australia, and Asia. The guy was definitely connected. Touraj was one of those bi-polar nuts, never remembering what he did and did not do. He buried himself in minutiae but never saw the big picture. Barry didn't want to know anything about anything. He provided the money. It was those two who contacted me about putting the whole project together. All I had to do was keep all the players focused on a common cause. The product sold itself.

Anyway, the major Saudi companies such as ARAMCO and PETROMIN immediately saw the technical benefits and bottom line payback. However, they wanted labels and literature in Arabic, and time to conduct a six-month field test; both reasonable requests. You see, doing business in KSA is much the same as in USA. The Saudi business owners are educated in UK and US, and they hire Brits and Americans to manage their companies.

My Stateside partners balked at both requirements, feeling (like many Americans) that the rest of the world should adapt to our standards and methods. Think about it; why are we the only country in the world not on the metric system? Geez, if you listened to that duffass Touraj, you'd think they still believe in flying carpets in the Middle East.

Neither were the Saudis totally innocent in this comic opera, the joke being mainly on me. They took the original contract we signed in California, had it rewritten in Arabic claiming it was the law of the land, and returned it to me for signatures. However, before I sent it back to the US, I had a Lebanese friend translate it for me. Turned out the Arabic version significantly put the screws to the American partners.

Chapter 10: The Last Cult

Sometime later I also found out the Americans were "value engineering" the original chemical formula, which would cost less to produce but penalize product performance. The good ol' tried and true bait-and-switch maneuver. Once again, a lesson learned: greed and politics seem to almost always trump principles; an unfortunate human condition.

I spent a lot of time cleaning up after Touraj. He had a tendency to call people with information either totally untrue or completely inaccurate. I guess he wanted to come off like a big cheese. Here's an example of a call I made to Newport Beach from Riyadh.

"Dammit, Touraj, why did you tell Amr that there is going to be a special formulation for guns?"

"I didn't."

"So Amr's lying to me?"

"I haven't spoken to Amr for two weeks."

"Touraj, I just spoke with him. He's three feet away from me. How about I put him on the speaker?"

"I gotta go. Important call coming in." He hangs up.

I called Barry to fill him in.

"Hey, you shithead, how's it going," he said in his best hail-fellow-well-met voice ending in a Bill Clintonesque haw-haw type giggle.

"Barry, you've got to get control of Touraj. He's fucking up everything." I was exasperated.

"Aw, he's just a dumb shit. Ignore him."

"That I can do, but you've got to stop him from calling everyone and scaring the crap out of them with his hallucinations."

Laughter. "Hallucinations, huh? That's a good one. What a dumb shit." More laughter. "Hey, did I tell you what's going on?"

I was almost afraid to ask. "No."

"Anyway, I ran into this retired Marine general who's going to help me take over the chemical company."

I was in a state of shock. "You mean to tell me while I'm over here busting my ass, you're going to attempt a hostile takeover of Buck's business?" I had to sit down.

"Yeah, isn't that a hoot?" More laughter.

So there it was: I flopped miserably as a team-builder, something I guaranteed all the players I could carry out with their cooperation. That they did not cooperate was of little consolation. I knew all about their duplicity and self-serving natures from the get-go, but thought I could "cure" them, forgetting that personality change comes only from psychoanalysis or religious conversion neither a field in which I was qualified. Frustrated and angry, I flew home a week before Christmas and milled around the house and mainly served as a major source of irritation for my wife, herself not too pleased at the months I spent away from home accomplishing nothing but putting us in an economic bind. I tried to think of methods for putting the project back together, but knew it was highly unlikely. In statistical terms it was possible but not probable.

One day in early February I received an unusual phone call. The caller was the general manager for a new factory being built near Austin, Texas for a telecom company based in the San Fernando Valley area of southern California.

"I'm really glad to catch you," said the caller, whose name was Allan. "I just finished your book, and you're just like we are." He seemed quite pleased.

Chapter 10: The Last Cult

I had written a book three years previously about leading the turnaround of a factory in Irvine, California. The theme was that the event was so transforming the rest of my life was a quest to find it again. Success of the book based on revenue was mediocre at best. You might say sales started off slow then tapered off. Needless to say, I was surprised by the call, and more surprised that my book was the cause of it.

"Anyway," said the caller cheerfully, "you should join us. I'm looking for an operations manager. Are you interested?"

What was there to lose? "Sure," I said. We agreed to meet the following Tuesday.

To make a long story short, when I arrived, the corporate vice president for human resources was also there. Their idea was that I *not* become the operations manager in Texas, but build and operate another factory in Indiana. That is, do the same thing as Allan. We reached a quick and amicable agreement.

I called Barry.

"Hey, I'm out; found something else to do," I said.

By May we wrapped up all the job details at the corporate office in California and I flew to Indianapolis with an air of contentment and optimism. Not only would I be paid quite well, I would also receive equity in the corporation.

During my time at the corporate office, I met the board members, the executive team, visited their factories and talked with everyone from management to floor sweepers. Everyone had a sense of pride and togetherness. Their motto was "We're all in this together," and they actually lived it. They were collectively the nicest bunch of business people I ever met. Later I discovered there was also a sinister undertone percolating beneath.

With that in mind, let me move ahead through the salad years. Four years later, we had factories in southern California, North Carolina, Texas, and Indiana, and were about to build in England and Northern California. Business was booming. In fact, business had doubled on an annual basis since the corporation formed in the early 1990s. I couldn't have been happier, congratulating myself on finally finding the job I had looked for all my life. The only thing somewhat concerning was the behavior of a few of my peers at corporate headquarters, but I was in denial; wanted to believe the best. Toward the end I learned that corporate was known throughout the sales organization as the Death Star.

During that period I received regular visits from my boss, the CEO, and his two main confidants, the vice president of human resources, Terry, and the vice president of engineering, Bill. Neither was needed on the operational level, but each had the function of assuring the corporate culture of "we're all in this together" was promoted and maintained. Well and good. However, and here's the sinister part, they both skulked around and recruited informants, not to discover what was going right, but to root out apostates. People who worked for me complained that they received after hours phone calls to see how "things were *really* going on around here." The corporate confidants searched high and low so they would have "something to report." They reminded me of the Communist Party morale officers who accompanied every command position in the old Red Army. Interestingly, the HR person was from Russia, having left the Motherland when she was ten years old. She was very nice on the outside, but drank to excess, and was always poking her nose into practically everything looking for "revisionism" (as defined by her own standards). She loved to have something negative to report to the CEO. That sure fits the Russian stereotype, and face it, folks, stereotypes are stereotypes for a reason. Do you suppose it's in their DNA?

Chapter 10: The Last Cult

Word got back to me during my first year on the job that it had been reported that I was trying to replace their culture with one of my own. That was news to me. I ignored it; let it slide. However, I noticed one disturbing pattern that at first I chalked up to real and justified concern on their part. Typically one of them, before departing for the west coast, would come into my office and close the door; a meaningful look and a sigh. . . .

"Bob is a good man, our kind…"

"Yes," I replied. "He is dedicated, does good work, and the folks like him."

"What do you think about Tim? Are you sure about him?"

"Of course," I said patiently, trying not to show any emotion, "or I wouldn't have hired him. He's busting his tail."

"Some people aren't sure he's right for us."

"What people?"

"I can't tell you that."

"Why not?"

"It's confidential."

"Wait a minute. I have bottom line responsibility for this operation, and these people work for me. How could anything that goes on here be confidential from me?"

Silence. Lack of eye contact. Squirming. They were not used to being questioned. It seemed I didn't know my place.

Sometimes I would receive a follow-up call from the CEO that informed me I had hurt the HR executive's feelings. Inside I was truly annoyed, but I had to give her credit; what a manipulator.

Talk about frustration. "Come on, Joe, I was completely reasonable in my request. Anyway, if women want to be executives they need to know there's no place for hurt feelings in business. We must use an economy of words and cut through the PC crap if our focus is business and not promoting some kind of social club."

You get the idea: typical corporate unasked for, buttinski "help," the idea being they controlled my operation, or at least tried to, not me. They worked relentlessly to covertly undermine me with my team, but it didn't work. As soon as I caught on to their game I put my folks on alert. Of course there were those exceptions, perhaps jealous of others, who felt a sense of power in being "chosen" by a corporate executive and would report their own spin, but I knew who they were. My own HR manager told me corporate HR controlled my operation, not me. I got rid of her skillfully manipulating corporate HR to administer the final blow, but that's another story.

The Indiana Operation turned out to be the most profitable in the corporation, producing the same amount of sales revenue as other operations, but with better margins. We also developed more new products than the other four operations combined. Life was good all across the company. Bonuses and profit sharing hit all time highs. An unexpected by-product of all this success was a creeping arrogance and head-in-the-sand denial of reality. Anyone who dared suggest our long-term strategy was off the mark was quickly branded to "have issues."

After record months, October and November, of a record year I challenged the forecasted revenue for the upcoming year. In addition to my other duties, I was the strategic planning facilitator for the corporation. As such, I kept my finger on the pulse of the market always evaluating what we did right, what we did wrong, and recommended what action should be taken on the difference.

Chapter 10: The Last Cult

"Our market cannot expand forever. I think it has hit the high, and we should focus on a strategy for a contracting market," I offered. "If I'm wrong we can always ramp up."

From the looks I received, one would have thought I farted in church.

"I've met with all our distributors," said the vice president of marketing, "and they have each increased their forecasts for next year."

"C'mon, Rich, I was at one of those meetings. The best I heard was that they would try to meet the goals you gave them. Surely you saw the eye-rolling that accompanied their response."

"We've always done better; always exceeded our forecast. Always!"

"Yeah, but why will that be likely next year? From what I can see the market is slowing, our products are not differentiated from Brand X, and we have more competitors than ever competing for share, some with very deep pockets that could pull a GE and buy the market."

The CFO piped up. "What does that mean, buy the market?" He made a face and snorted.

"When GE's patent ran out on synthetic diamond for grinding wheels, all sorts of competitors jumped in. GE thumbed their nose and reduced price from eight dollars a carat to eighteen cents a carat; ran everyone else out of business. They bought the market."

"Look," pleaded Rich. "Building after building of data room hotels are under construction because businesses don't want their own data rooms anymore. They want to outsource the whole operation."

"Who says?"

"All the big datacom and telecom companies."

"But not the end-users." I said it as a statement not a question.

Rich made a face. "No, the market outlook mostly comes from our distributors."

"Have you seen data or is this some kind of tribal knowledge?" I was becoming very unpopular in the room.

Silence. They had no market research data, only their own myopic view of the world. They had become victims of their own success. They were convinced that our products, undifferentiated though more expensive, were preferred because we were "better people."

I pressed on. "I shouldn't have to tell you what kind of trouble we can get into with a build-it-and-they-will-come attitude and strategy."

"Why not?" said the CEO. "It's always worked before."

"The past does not always predict the future," I began. "And we as managers can only be value-added to the company in two ways: first by getting roadblocks out of the way of those actually doing something, and secondly by being adequate in the major part of our job: prediction."

They didn't like the lecture. Uh-oh, I now had "issues."

Three months later, the market did slow, and we had to pull the plug on the potential UK operation. We'd spent six million dollars mainly renting facilities, hiring managers, traveling back and forth and interviewing support people. Those interviews were not for listening, but for telling the interviewees how great we were. We made no plans to convert our products, drawings, and documents to the metric system; even though we were told in no uncertain terms metric conversion was an absolute necessity. That's right: our stuff is so good the

Chapter 10: The Last Cult

rest of the world will be happy to accept it as is. Talk about unintended arrogance and learned ignorance; or were they just clueless?

We also committed just short of one-hundred million dollars into erecting a state-of-the-art northern California plant that would never open. Before it was completed we were seeking a buyer.

Then came the wake up call of September 11, 2001.

The entire executive staff was in my conference room when the news broke. I should mention at this point that we had rotating executive staff meetings every six weeks. The agenda was always massive and the participants became mired in circuitous minutiae. The prevailing tone was to avoid any decision; engage in further study until next meeting and on and on. This also applied to no-brainer black and white items. (The CEO said there was no such thing as a "no-brainer.") The North Carolina general manager once whispered to me the objective was to drive everything to gray. Suddenly the agenda driven minutiae wasn't important anymore. The group scattered immediately seeking ways home. Airports, bus stations, and train depots were all a mess.

Over the next six months the market for telecom non-active hardware continued to contract. For the first time, the company faced an economical crisis. I led the group in what was to be my final strategic planning session. The verdict was to get rid of the corporate headquarters and one or two operations. Although my operation was the most profitable, it was chosen. This meant I would fall on my sword as well.

I said my good-bye in the CEO's office in Westlake Village, California. Even with the mildly sinister undercurrent, I loved the job and the people. I would miss them.

"What are you thinking of doing now?" he said.

"I don't know, Joe. Haven't thought much about it. Maybe get back to writing; work on a few projects—not sure. Have to let the dust settle awhile."

"I know this company meant a lot to you."

"True enough."

"Want to have lunch?" He was eager to show off his new T-bird.

"No, I think I'll head to the airport; get an earlier flight. We've got a lot to do to shut down the plant and transfer product lines in the next sixty days."

"How about I send some help?" I knew he meant his two cronies, who would basically be there to spy and report.

"No, thanks."

Guess what? They showed up anyway. A predictable ending to a bizarre adventure. What a ride.

Chapter 11

Class of '58 Lounge

I GRADUATED from Defiance High School around the first day of June 1958. Originally the site of General "Mad" Anthony Wayne's Fort Defiance, the town is located at the confluence of the Auglaize and Maumee Rivers in the northwest corner of Ohio, about an hour south of Toledo and forty-five minutes east of Fort Wayne, Indiana. At that time, the population was about twelve thousand souls. The area is green, wooded, and occupied by numerous forty-acre farms. In addition, light-industry factories abound, mainly producing small parts for General Motors, Ford, Chrysler, and the automotive after-market.

The largest employer in Defiance, since 1950, is a General Motors gray iron foundry located just outside the eastern city limits. Though recent years have been fraught with uncertainty, lay-offs, downsizing, and (in the case of GM) union bumping from closed factories in Michigan, 1958 was the middle of an economic boom. Optimism abounded.

Everyone liked Ike (who visited Defiance twice during the 1950s), Vince Lombardi was building a dynasty in Green

Chapter 11: Class of '58 Lounge

Bay, the Browns were winning in Cleveland, and the Big Ten ruled college football. Americans loved winners. So did Defiance, Ohio.

The DHS Class of 1958 did not measure up to expectations of faculty, school board, and community. We were considered in the same breath as other hapless underachievers (losers) of the era: Chicago Cardinals, St. Louis Browns, Boston Bruins, Adlai E. Stevenson, and Nash Automobiles, to name a few.

Claude W. Henkle, Superintendent of Defiance County Schools, and former Principal of DHS, made this remark to a group of faculty members: "That class is the worst in the history of Defiance High School."

Well, maybe so, but we looked successful in the sense of a typical magazine layout. You know the look: bright, freshly-scrubbed, athletic young men and women charging off to college and the military to perpetuate the American dream. Though the Class of '58 was a disappointment to administrators and faculty, *we were not a disappointment to ourselves*. We considered ourselves to be "normal" teen-aged students. Sure, spurred by Henkle's negative endorsement, teachers told us, from the ninth grade on, we were making history for being eight-balls, but (being concrete heads) we ignored those comments—actually took a bit of pride in being the best in something, even if it was in being the worst. That makes a kind of sideways thinking sense, doesn't it? Hell, we reasoned, they were just trying to motivate us to work harder—probably told that to every class. And anyway, the teachers most critical of us we considered bozos. You know what I mean, the kind who taught school because they couldn't get a "regular" job; at least that's how we rationalized our assessment.

All of their criticism was aimed (rightly so) at the boys. Say, I just got a flash! Maybe that's why the girls in our class wouldn't date us! Oh sure, there were exceptions, but those guys were goody-goody, brown-noser types. Come to think about it, I can't believe those girls were so short-sighted, didn't fall all over us, us being the only guys on the planet that understood the real geometry of the universe coupled with such a cool worldview. I guess we were before our time—paradigm pioneers. Yeah, that's it. It's like the rest of the world was out of step with us, know what I mean?

My younger brothers said the town and academics were still talking about us when they were juniors and seniors. We were the example of what not to do. The main theme seemed to be that we were the worst students, worst athletes, worst citizens, worst mannered, the least ambitious, and the biggest collection of smart alecks ever turned on humanity in one concentrated group. I suppose I should explain that we were not mean, destructive, or evil—just high-spirited and in some cosmic way tightly connected to each other. Daily study hall activities included squirt guns, spit wads, or rubber band sling shots depending on the "season." We also waged bean (or pea) shooter wars, sailed blown-up condoms out of windows, and participated in loud belching or (better still) audible flatulence (the louder the better). The key word is *daily*, not occasionally, seldom, or once-in-a-while. There are many specific examples I could cite. Too many. Here are a few examples that do not violate *minimum* standards of decency, though some may push the envelope.

During the "season," nightly raids were made by any number of marauders on fruit orchards and watermelon patches. This sometimes drew gun fire from the farmers. Their ammo was rock salt fired from a shotgun. I heard it stung like hell.

Some of us preferred shoplifting forays at downtown grocery stores just for the challenge of getting something for nothing. Watermelon season was especially rewarding. Shopkeepers conveniently stacked them in front of the stores like

Chapter 11: Class of '58 Lounge

cannon balls. One guy played quarterback while a number of halfbacks ran by and received handoffs.

One of my favorite pranks was water ballooning vehicles at night. This was either accomplished at roadside if we wanted the thrill of a chase ("You little son of a bitch, I'm going to kill you."), or atop a railroad overpass if we wanted the victim to be utterly confused. They never looked up even though we should have given ourselves away with helpless giggling. We even bombed police cars. They were as clueless as the rest. Their heads swiveled all over the place, but they never looked up.

Once in a while we shelled a faculty member's house with rotten fruit, usually after one of us was unfairly accused of wrongdoing. The following morning an announcement was made over the public address system demanding the vandals report to the principal's office immediately. The final remark was a sinister, "We know who you are!" We never fell for that one. After a day or two of zero results, they would round up "the usual suspects," which could have been any group of three or four from the Class of '58. Then came, in succession, the third degree, threats, and promises of amnesty if you would rat out the culprits. We never fell for those tricks either.

Some preferred to stamp a provocative word or phrase from end zone to end zone the length of the football field during winter snows. Many of the classrooms overlooked the field.

"Will the boys who are responsible for the football field report to the office. We know who you are!" Right.

Other study hall disruptions (these rooms were huge halls, probably the size of four regular classrooms) featured rolling marbles down the wooden floor, a loud fart, and/or a window rattling belch from the hallway just outside. You see, the acoustics and reverberations were outstanding from the closed hallways constructed of tile floors, walls, and ceiling. Some enterprising lads outside taking physical education threw eggs, clods, or rocks through the open second and third story windows. (No air-conditioning then, sports fans.)

As you can see, this was just typical boys-will-be-boys stuff common to practically all generations. However, the Class of '58 was distinguished because 1) practically everyone took part, and 2) the frequency of these events was almost constant.

Ah, I remember it as if it were yesterday... it was the ninth grade, second period study hall just before the bell... Sharon, an attractive, popular-type classmate sat directly behind Percy. I occupied the desk directly to Sharon's left. Sharon generally ignored us, but managed to convey the impression she smelled bad cheese when we caught her eye. Just before the bell rang for the beginning of the period and silence, Percy turned around, grinned at Sharon, and let go with probably the loudest and juiciest blast of intestinal vapor heard on the earth to this day. It was definitely a classic. "Oh, my God!" Sharon blurted with a gagging, horrified look on her face. I laughed so hard that control of my bladder was in doubt.

One activity that was very popular with some of my classmates, though not with me, was window-peeking on girls during their evening baths. Others of us spent our evenings lifting cases of clinking, wet refreshment from Coke delivery trucks to trade at certain grocery stores for "water" balloons. (See, in those days the sides weren't enclosed.) Back to the voyeurs: They were well-organized and shared data about who, where, and what time to develop a schedule and avoid getting in each other's way. I suspect they learned more about teamwork from this nightly exercise than they did participating on athletic teams. There, the coaches just shouted with vein-popping gusto and cursed our ineptitude. Anyway, Danny and Gary probably came up with the most difficult voyeurism.

Chapter 11: Class of '58 Lounge

Some gymnastic skill was needed. It required using a wooden box (strategically hidden for the occasion) to get atop a fence to mount a steeply pitched roof where one was required to hang upside down to get a perfect view into the bathtub of one of our princesses.

Academic standing did not disqualify one from participating in our shenanigans. John was studious and won an appointment to West Point. The guy could smell up the school library better than most, but never received the blame because "John wouldn't do something like that." However, Lloyd, the school librarian, a cheesy, little, effeminate-acting flamer, revoked the library cards of the rest of us. Lloyd spoke in a high-pitched, nasal voice and said things like, "Oh, good heavens!" and "Oh, my goodness gracious!" We finally got banned from the library for good midway through our senior year when we discovered Lloyd's secret cache of Pecan Sandies, which we greedily devoured. Back to John: In a seventh period study hall, he won the admiration of many and elicited a piercing shriek from Danny that, of course, brought down the house. John turned in his seat and wiped a humongous, multi-colored booger on Danny's homework. Danny's disturbance cost him two periods in detention, while those of us who laughed each received one. John? He received none because "John wouldn't do something like that."

One final good-natured poke directed at the administrators was delivered during Senior Day, a variety show staged by graduating seniors for the entire school and community, which occurred the final day of classes.

The Senior Day Committee consisted of some "good-standing" classmates and was chaired by Mr. Green, a faculty member and senior class advisor. They alone decided the show's theme and auditioned the prospective acts. Mr. Green made a Puritan seem liberal. Most acts deemed acceptable featured bland, record-pantomiming groups mouthing hits of the day (e.g., "How Much Is That Doggie in the Window?") and cavorting about thinking they were amusing. Absolute rubbish! Mr. Green censored a trio of girls (who actually sang) because the boy accompanying them on rhythm guitar was of dubious character. Unable to find a suitable replacement, the trio had to perform a cappella. With that in mind, and of being of dubious character ourselves, Bob and I staged a bit of a ruse to get accepted.

We showed up at the audition billing ourselves as a hillbilly duet called the Avery Brothers, Alex and Eugene, and sang an harmless but entertaining little ditty called, "Listen to the Gooney Bird." Earlier, Bob found a guitar at home and I borrowed one from the school. We taught ourselves a few basic chords, a bit of vocal harmony and rehearsed our asses off. The committee not only found us acceptable, they decided to anchor the show with our act hitting in the clean-up slot; that is, performing the closing number.

We then began rehearsing a different song for the show, "Little Ol' Kiss O' Fire," a parody of Kay Starr's "Kiss of Fire." Although it was also basically harmless, we knew Mr. Green would veto any song with kissing in the theme, but we liked it better and knew our audience would as well. I should also explain that we selected our name because it sounded like a popular duo of the time, the Everly Brothers; however, in reality Alex and Eugene Avery were actually local dull-witted dropouts who graduated from juvenile delinquency to hooliganism. Neither Mr. Green nor the committee had a clue, them being disconnected from the mainstream student body. They were Brahmans, so how could they know?

The day of the show Bob and I were hanging out at lunch with a dozen or so of our classmates. My best buddy, Dennis, and Larry suggested everyone zip downtown quickly and purchase groceries to throw at us at the end of our act. The idea quickly got legs and spread to almost all of our male

Chapter 11: Class of '58 Lounge

classmates. Since seniors attended the performance in cap and gown, it was no trouble smuggling the ammo into the theater.

The theme was a televised dance show, a la *American Bandstand*, with the emcee playing Dick Clark, and couples dressed to the nines on stage. When "Dick" introduced each act, the couples left the dance floor to sit at tables on stage. Bob and I rehearsed our number backstage probably twenty times. Finally we were announced.

"Please welcome Alex and Eugene, the Avery Brothers!"

From the back of the theater came some laughter from those who got the joke, followed by thunderous, overly generous applause—clearly word had spread and many knew what was coming. Bob noisily and ineptly fumbled around with a music stand and some faux sheet music, and I put a sign on the front of the stand. In large block letters it said, MEN with a directional pointing arrow beneath. Laughter. Feigning embarrassment, we looked at the sign and turned it around. THE AVERY BROTHERS. More laughter; more got the joke. The couples on stage and "Dick Clark" (all from the committee) seemed confused. We strummed our guitars, and began in our best hillbilly twang.

> *I touch your lips that's when the trouble starts a-brewin'*
> *I cain't resist the brand tobacco you are chewin'...*

At the end of the second verse, Bob started picking and strumming his guitar with maniacal fervor. I stopped and said,

"Hey, Alex, you playin' what's written?"

"No, Eugene, ah'm playin' what's rotten!"

More laughter. Several verses and a chorus later including a quite inventive yodel (or so we were later told), we concluded by throwing in a key change to correctly time the syllables for the final two lines.

And when you kiss me you set my mouth on fire,
That burns that cigar and your little ol' kiss o' fire.

When the applause died down, I stepped to the microphone and looked into the front center section where the seniors sat. Damned near every male in the class was reaching beneath his gown and grinning maliciously. I glanced at Bob. He whispered with a giggle, "Those bastards are going to try and bean us!"

I looked at him and smiled, "I know."

I looked into the crowd again and said, "Thank you! Would you like to hear another one?"

A loud chorus of "NO!!!" was followed by an absolute barrage of fruits and vegetables that sailed over and around Bob and me. Miraculously, not a one hit us. I recognized carrots, peaches, whole cabbages, but mostly juicy over-ripe tomatoes. The emcee and the couples behind us scurried for cover.

Before our senior trip, Bob and I were summoned to the class advisor's office and told it would cost three-hundred dollars to clean the backdrop that had been soiled by the thrown produce. Further, the money would be deducted from our class treasury, which would "penalize" the whole class for our selfishness and thoughtlessness. We pretended to give a damn. Predictably, when we looked at each other we cracked up with helpless laughter. Poor Mr. Green was seething, but what could he do?

***

And there you have it; a quick snapshot in time that describes the Defiance High School Class of 1958. Many went on to very successful and financially rewarding careers. A few are even rather famous. In that regard, the Class of '58 probably distinguished itself more than most. It has been common over the years to see several on CNN and read about others in

Chapter 11: Class of '58 Lounge

books, magazines, and newspapers. I think we also have four or five published authors. Not bad for a group of misfits, smart alecks, and ne'er-do-wells.

You could say I am quite fond of my classmates. Whenever I see one, it's as if the 1958 school year never ended. I remain convinced that the bond among us was very rare and special.

So, what do my high school memories have to do with the after hours adventures of an international businessman? Well boys and girls, I needed to provide this background to describe one such adventure that took place in the late 1990's in Greenfield, Indiana, birthplace and home of perhaps America's greatest poet, James Whitcomb Riley.

I had recently returned from a year in Saudi Arabia, and was contracted by a southern California manufacturer to build a factory in a nearby New Castle. Turned out, the only motel in that town, some thirty minutes away, was booked so I holed up in Greenfield at Lee's Inn near State Road 9 and Interstate 70.

After business hours one weekday, I was cruising down the main drag in Greenfield looking for a health club and a restaurant. The prospects were bleak. Earlier, I asked the desk clerk at the motel about a place to work out and a recommendation for a nice restaurant, and she looked at me like I was some kind of head case. Upon recollection, I should have known better. The girl was in her early twenties, but already had a body forty pounds over the legal road limit accompanied by a whiny personality that made her even more unattractive.

"Y'all mean like one o' them there gymnasiums, and like a Big Boy?" she cracked her gum and displayed a smoker's blackish tongue.

"Yeah, a gym or athletic club. Someplace with weight machines, treadmills; that sort of stuff. I'm looking for something a bit nicer than a Big Boy for dinner. Are there any local steakhouses?"

"Folks from around here don't have no call for a gym. Everybody works seven days a week," she said, pulling a strand of greasy hair from her shiny forehead. Several zits needed popped. "If'n they don't work seven days or two jobs, then they's likely laid off. Anyways, we don't need no gym."

"Uh, okay; what about a restaurant?"

"Just Big Boy, KFC, some pizza joints, and coupla great buffet places. All you can eat, and real cheap too."

"That's it?"

"'Fraid so."

This translated into fast-food joints or local places that had all-you-can-eat salad bars and buffets featuring wilted lettuce, rubbery carrots, and greasy, overly-breaded chicken-fried steak, deep-fried "stuff" (Roast beast? Seagull?), plenty of vein-clogging gravy, biscuits, sticky gelatinous desserts, and gooey mashed potatoes—all rather insipid. But, you get plenty of it—cheap!!! Hell of a deal!

I drove past Riley Hospital. I could imagine it clearly: the receptionist had to be a chain-smoker, and the ambulance probably had a standard transmission. Just as I was about to resign myself to turning into flab and instantly gaining thirty pounds, I saw "it." Note: Here one needs to mentally cue halleluiah-type choir music and heavenly light descending on the object of my attention. Got it? It was...

The Class of '58 Lounge!!!

Whoa! This had to be an omen. Naturally, I pulled into the parking lot and practically ran to the door.

The outside wasn't remarkable by any stretch of one's imagination, a storefront in a strip mall. No windows, just a

Chapter 11: Class of '58 Lounge

front door. I entered half expecting to see some of my classmates. At worse, maybe there would be people from some other class of 1958. Maybe they would be like us, you know? One never knows, does one?

No such luck. The place was filled with cigarette smoke; I mean *really* filled with cigarette smoke. One inhalation probably equaled a pack and a half a day dosage. When my stinging eyes adjusted to the dark, bar-room gloom, I made out the form of a good-sized, horseshoe-shaped bar. Only three stools (at the base of the horseshoe) were unoccupied, so I hopped on the one in the center. People that could be anywhere in age from late thirties to late forties surrounded me. With saloon denizens it's hard to tell. The environment has a definite aging component. Everyone except me was smoking. It seemed like their cigarettes were all about three inches long. New ones. Over the next gasping hour, every time I looked, all of the cancer-sticks were three inches long. Damn! Is there some kind of new "eternal" brand?

Another thing, everyone sort of looked the same—you know, like cousins. The uniform of the day was tank top shirts and shorts. The men all wore baseball caps advertising heavy equipment, farm implement manufacturers, truck brands or beer. Both sexes were built the same; solid piano-type legs, supporting an overweight, barrel-shaped torso. There was a lot of excess weight around the middle, but not what one would call potbellies. Maybe a good term is semi-lard. Yeah, that's it: there was a roomful of semi-lards. The guys had definite rolls, and the ladies had flab hanging from their arms where triceps should be. Men and women alike had at least sixteen-inch necks. In fact, the shape of their heads and necks resembled buckets turned upside down. Because of their upper body bulk, their arms could not hang straight down. Instead, they protruded from their shoulders at a forty-five degree angle down to the elbows and then straight down. The language was terrible.

One guy with a high-pitched voice that carried over the bar-room din complained that most of the women who tried to hit on him were *dirtbags*. Apparently, none of these dirtbags were present (could've fooled me) because no female tried to hit on him in the Class of '58 Lounge. The other guys loudly and profanely agreed they had the same problem. The women nodded knowingly. It was hard for me to imagine any woman attracted to this crew, but I could be wrong. I've seen some strange pairings out there, folks. Looking around the room and the available (excuse the expression) ladies, I'd like to see what they call a dirtbag. Probably a Schnauzer with a wig or something like that. In fact, it was pretty amazing that these guys would call anyone by that term, if you know what I mean, them being such attractive gentlemen themselves.

The most popular drink was beer, mostly Budweiser, but Jack Daniel's with Coke was a close second. The guy to my immediate right was puffing a cigarette so aggressively that you couldn't make out his head through the haze. The one with the dirtbag problem waddled up to him, and began a spirited discussion about baseball hats. It went something like this:

"Dammit, you sumbitch, you better get me one o' them there Lone Star Cement (pronounced see-ment) hats. And ah don' want none o' them plain red ones neither. You best git me one o' them there red velvet ones. Y'see ah'm wearin' mah blue one now, and ah already got me a plain red one. Use it for golf."

"Ah, bullshit. Blow it out yer ass. I cain't git no more hats from them. A hain't wantin' to see 'em no more. Leastwise, not no time soon." He blew a cool-looking smoke ring.

A semi-lard female walked up and started hanging on the first guy's shoulder. A visual of the two doing the nasty

Chapter 11: Class of '58 Lounge

flashed before me and gave me the willies. "Ah'm warnin' you dammit; you owe me one sure as shit!"

"Ah, bullshit! Ah don' owe you shit!"

"Fuckin' A! Ah gave you a Mack baseball hat last Christmas, you shithead! You owe me!"

The second guy takes a pull on his beer and lights up a new one. "Ah, bullshit, a gift's a gift. Ain't no call to repay a gift!" (Motions to the bartender for another beer and indicates to put it on the first guy's tab.)

"Shit there ain't!"

"Shit there is!"

"Okay, you sumbitch, now ah'm pissed. Ah'm gittin' even. EVERYBODY HEAR THAT? AH'M GITTIN' FUCKIN' EVEN!"

"Shee-it!"

"Just you wait. Someday yer gonna be wantin' me to pour some see-ment for you. And it's gonna be some bad shit. Just you wait!"

"You ain't never pourin' no see-ment for me agin. No fuckin' way!"

"That's what you think. You cain't never remember shit. You'll fergit. Just wait. Ah'll fix yer ass." Well, you get the idea. This conversation never ended during the time I was there. It only got louder and more profane, including some references to some particular anatomical impossibilities. Anyway, I can't recall much more. I was close to passing out from the combination of smells and smoke. Sometime during the great debate, I lost control of myself and ordered another beer and a greasy hamburger. I think the bartender offered it with an extra scoop of Crisco, but I refused.

Feeling compelled to wash my hands before handling the chopped beef delight, I made the mistake of seeking the men's restroom. The stench was overpowering, a combination of all the odors from the bar area combined with the unique bouquet of urine and bowel movements past. The sink was filthy, there was neither soap nor paper towels, remnants of toilet paper were all over the floor and walls, and the floor itself was completely wet and skuzzy, covered with numerous alien pubic hairs. I was repulsed by the fact my worn out (fortunately) running shoes were in contact with it and made a mental note to jettison them to the trash when I removed them later that night. The water level on the floor beneath the urinal looked especially deep, so rather than risk slipping (and an unwanted "swim"), I checked out the stall. The stool looked like something was growing on it, and it contained an unflushed septic log, but *no* accompanying toilet paper. I hoped the cook hadn't been the last occupant. I decided to eat my meal with unwashed hands (I mean, what's the point?) and pushed the door open with my elbow.

The hamburger arrived and proved to be a very tasty and satisfying gut bomb. I knew the odor of grilled onions, slimy meat, and past-the-expiration-date mustard would be impregnated into my hands for days. As I fought off the volcanic emergence of a belch with a swig of beer, I noticed that a newly arrived couple was perched at the horseshoe bar to my right. These new arrivals did not look like the rest of the customers except the man wore a baseball cap. They were considerably older than the rest of the crowd, probably between late seventies and early eighties. Now I didn't feel quite so out of place as being the only "different" person in the house. And, you know, I really resented being in an establishment that included the words Class of '58 and feeling so out of place. I wanted to fit in, but realized the fact that I didn't was because of *me*, not them.

Chapter 11: Class of '58 Lounge

After I puzzled a bit about that, I recognized it was the same feeling I had at our last class reunion, which was so disconcerting I vowed never to return for another. That barstool reflection provided a genuine eureka-type moment. It was *me*, not my classmates. *I* was the different one; the square peg. It was I who no longer fit.

My concentration was momentarily diverted from the couple, and my reverie, to scarf another mouthful of the gut bomb. When I glanced back, both were smoking three-inch long cigarettes. He was drinking a boilermaker, and she was playing the pinball machine with gusto and art. I mean, she was really smacking that machine around, making the universe comply with her internal desire, and yet avoiding the dreading tilt shutdown. Not only that, she was swearing like a sailor as she made the shiny, steel sphere dance about racking up points at warp speed rate.

"Shit, not bad," grunted her spouse.

"You betcher ass," she replied.

Rats. Alone and out of place again.

I paid my bill and rose to leave. No one paid any attention to my departure. In fact, everyone seemed to be pointedly ignoring me from the time I walked in. I even had to hail the barkeep several times to get served, and again to pay my bill.

The message was driven home for a second time. I was different. I didn't belong, and thank God for that. Again a reality moment: I no longer completely fit in with my former classmates either; a variation on the theme than "one cannot go home again." Even though I made a *vital few* lifetime friends and shared many great juvenile escapades, I realized the *trivial many* and I no longer had much in common. Upon further reflection, I realized the paths of our developing worldviews significantly diverged as we neared graduation. For instance: Most of them talked about getting shop-rat type jobs or joining the military. Me, I wanted to get educated and see the world. They planned marriages; I preferred to remain single. Hell, I neither dated nor made close friends with any girl of my graduating class. My classmates also evolved to become more "adult" meaning serious-minded, while I remained a "kid" always pursuing amusement, which is still the case.

I walked out the door into a quiet evening filled with fresh air. I could almost see the noxious fumes from the Class of '58 Lounge rise from my clothing and foul the environment. I hoped this was not a cruel metaphor played by some evil spirit; a place set down on earth for only two hours to capture my soul. Another message was additionally clear: 1958 was in the past and probably best left there. Except the best part; the part that is in my mind. But... let me dwell on that for a moment.

You see, life is a gift that must be given back, and joy should arise from its possession. I've always conspired to squeeze joy from every second, and cheat time by keeping fit and adapting to new trends and technology. Now, I know this is a battle that must be lost, but any fight to maintain or increase joy is still noble, isn't it? The year 1958 fits into my personal fantasy world where I am forever young and the future has no limit. On the other hand, today I can see the finish line; the end of everything, which truth to tell I resent. But joy is not decreased, only counted sorrow. Sorrow for the joy filled days that I'll miss when on that one fateful day I'll pass beyond the veil of this life and into the shadows of Sheol.

The Class of '58 Lounge offered a door to my youthful past, and I eagerly ran through it. Anticipation turned to disappointment (life can double-cross with style), but I'd do it again just to see what's on the other side.

Some have called me an impractical dreamer unwilling to face reality, but I assure you, dear reader, that is not the case. I subscribe to the Dennis Miller theory that life after high school

Chapter 11: Class of '58 Lounge

is a fifty to sixty year episode of occasional kicks to the groin; that we have to learn to survive on a Serengeti Plain populated with leopards. However, I also celebrate vintage memories whenever they appear, especially those from that innocent age when my fellow time travelers and I knew each other by heart. And I'm always eager to return.

Okay, so maybe I am a bit of a dreamer. Oh, and I attended our fiftieth class reunion and had a wonderful time.

Afterword

I CONTINUE to travel for business, though not nearly as often, and have continued to experience and enjoy the fall-out from outside, serendipitous circumstances. When looking through the lens of joy, you could say that all my business trips are also pleasure trips.

My friend, Chuck, from *Around the World in Forty Days*, felt a twinge when weight training, which quickly became excruciating pain that eventually subsided. Thinking his physical body had returned to normal, he followed the normal flow of traffic at seventy-five mph on I-45 to his office when he was struck blind. Somehow he guided his automobile to safety on the roadside when the pain returned. His sight returned a bit later.

I visited him in Houston six months after the attack. He told me they were controlling his affliction with massive doses of steroids and other drugs. The strong, robust, bigger-than-life guy I knew was a balding shell who could barely walk. His physicians told him he has a good chance of surviving four more years. However, other than seeking God, he has the same cheerful, optimistic personality.

The last thing he said was that maybe we could play tennis again in six months. I hope he's right.